Are You Parenting the Adult of the Future?

A Practical Guide of 7 Life Skills of the Future to Prepare Your Teenager and Child

Dina Dimitriou, MA, MBPsS

Dedication

To my mum and dad, thank you. I only understood your sacrifice and selflessness when I became a mum. I love you.

Table of Contents

Introduction

We've all heard our parents' generation firmly state, "Well, back in my day, kids played outside all day long without supervision and we turned out just fine!" Usually, the comment is said with a look of disdain, followed quickly with a comment about how kids these days are too coddled to take care of themselves and that it's a wonder they can do anything right. Even between our parents' and our children's generations, so much has changed that the two experiences are hardly comparable.

The world has changed. We're now more aware than ever about the dangers of letting children ride in the truck bed without any sort of restraints, or roaming freely. While the world has never been a safer place, statistically speaking, we're all too aware of the dangers lurking around every corner and with every choice we make, we do what we can to mitigate that risk. Of course, our parents look at us as we parent our own children like we're overbearing and like we're trying to infantilize our children, but when you know better, you do better.

However, while parents are busy taking care of their children's ever-changing physical and academic needs, there is one area that is sorely lacking: Mental health. Often, there's such an emphasis on raising children to be ready for adulthood and to have a healthy body that it's easy to forget essential lessons in life that aren't taught in school. School teaches children to answer questions and work within certain constraints of the world, preparing them for a lifetime of working. However, this isn't a foundation for mental health. The foundation for a healthy mindset begins early and requires skills that the traditional education system has not been particularly good at fostering.

Our children are only children for so long. We only have a few short years where we as parents can influence our children as they enter adulthood. There are so many lessons out there that our children need to learn that parents completely forget about because they struggle with them themselves! However, mentally healthy parents can help foster mental wellness in children as well; and that will go a long way in creating happy, healthy, resilient adults in the future.

Life isn't about who can be the smartest person or who makes the most money or who has the nicest things; it's about happiness. It's about feeling fulfilled, comfortable in one's own skin, and ready to face the day—no matter what that day will bring. This is fostered through having mindsets geared toward positivity. Some call it emotional intelligence. To others, it's resilience. To me, it's mental wellness.

By focusing on habits that will create health and mental wellness, children will be equipped to endure the world of tomorrow. We have no way of knowing what the world will be like when the children of today enter adulthood, but what we can do is teach them tried and true strategies and mindsets that will take them far. The key to being able to teach those lessons to children is to have parents who lead by example. You are the most important person in your child's life in regards to shaping them into their adult selves. Your child will look to you, learn from you, and emulate you every step of the way. By ensuring that you, yourself, are mentally well and have healthy mindsets, you dramatically increase the likelihood that your child will as well. The world will be different when your child faces it alone, but one thing is for sure: The mental tools necessary for success will remain the same.

As you read through this book, we will establish seven key traits that both you and your children should try to apply to your everyday life: Resilience, a growth mindset, self-compassion, mindfulness, creativity, sustainability, and gratitude. Each of these traits, when implemented early on, will help to prepare your child for anything that comes his or her way.

We will be focusing on two key aspects for each and every trait: How to develop it for you, the parent, and how to foster that trait in your children as well. Resilience will help your child feel empowered to continue seeking a solution, no matter the problem. A growth mindset reminds your child that they're always capable of learning. It is to recognize that we all may make mistakes, but those mistakes serve as valuable lessons that we can learn from. Failure and mistakes aren't the end of the world, and rather serve as ways that we can learn and grow as people. Self-compassion ensures that your child doesn't become his or her worst enemy through criticism. Mindfulness keeps your child grounded and able to cope with all sorts of problems. Creativity works to help with problem solving. Sustainability protects the world that we all live in, protecting the environment.

Finally, gratitude reminds us all that we should be thankful for what we have instead.

As you know better, you do better. Recognizing the value of these seven life skills means that you'll also recognize the importance of the implementation. Hopefully, as you begin implementing these strategies, you'll start seeing a difference in your child as well. There will be plenty of tips, tricks, and activities that can be used to help along the way as well, from taking mindful walks together, implementing gratitude at dinner each night, and more.

These skills are the very ones that I recommend to my own clients. As a coaching psychologist who focuses primarily on working with both parents and teenagers, I've emphasized resilience and mindfulness in my practice. I care about bringing peace between parent and child by encouraging the development of habits and skills that will enable both to feel heard, positive, and healthy. The relationship between parent and child can be a tricky one, especially as the child grows and recognizes that there is an inherent disconnect between the two just due to the different viewpoints they have. You see the world inherently differently than your child does.

However, despite this difference, the skills necessary to cope with the world remain the same.

Remember that these life skills are meant to last a lifetime. They may be difficult to implement at first, but over time, they will get easier. The first time that you try to mindfully ground yourself after you just heard your furious teen scream that she hates you or that you're a horrible parent will be difficult; but over time, these skills will become easier. Over time, they will become much more natural to you and you will be able to find that success in a more simple way as well.

It is my hope that the information that I provide will help you to foster a closer relationship with yourself and your children, while also providing skills that will prepare you for the real world. It is easy to get caught up with thinking of parenting as being within a bubble—you take care of your child reactively rather than proactively. You react and correct behaviors instead of encouraging positive mindset and behaviors ahead of time. In shifting to this more proactive mindset, you will be providing your child with tools to cope with conflict, disappointment, and other adversities. You will teach your child how to approach the world in a healthier manner that will be sustainable, beneficial, and enjoyable. As an added bonus, you get to enjoy the same benefits by implementing them into your own life.

Chapter One: Bend, Don't Break: The Power of Adaptability, Flexibility and Resilience

This life we live is full of all sorts of challenges. Things don't always go according to plan. You may think that you're ready for something, only to have it go wrong. Maybe you were set to go on a road trip, only to realize that you have a flat tire that is preventing you from doing so. Maybe you were going to an interview and spilled coffee all over your clothes. As an adult, you know just how frustrating these sorts of things can be. You know the struggles of trying to cope with the tumultuous emotions that come as a result. This is learned through your own life experience—you know that things don't always work out the way you expected; and you learn to sort of roll with the punches.

Children and teenagers have much less experience in doing this. They may lack the experience that tells them that they can't always plan on things working out for them. This is why when younger children drop their ice cream cone that they've been waiting for in line for the last 15 minutes, they get so upset. The world didn't go according to plan and they are upset. You might be rolling your eyes at the fact that your child is crying over something so small when it really isn't that big of a deal to go back through the line and get a replacement. But, your child is acting like it's the end of the world.

To your child, it *is* the end of the world. What doesn't matter much to you—because in the grand scheme of things, it's not a big deal—is hugely important to your child who may not have the life experience of dealing with problems to understand that there are better ways to cope. Teenagers also have less life experience than you and will react poorly if things don't quite work out for them and they don't have the tools in place to help cope. They may not necessarily start crying when something goes wrong; but they may feel lost, anxious, and unsure what to do, and that can quickly lend itself to lashing out in frustration or anger that usually only serves to make things worse.

One of the best things that you can do for your children is to ensure that they understand how to cope with adversity before they have to deal with it. It starts small—teaching your child how to deal with the disappointment of a tower of blocks falling down. And as it builds up, your child slowly builds up the important skills necessary for coping when life gets a bit messy.

The Importance of Adaptability, Flexibility, and Resilience

Adaptability, flexibility, and resilience all may seem like the same thing, but they are a bit different. They all contribute to creating a mindset that will be capable of coping with adversity and challenges, but they all do so in different ways. Adaptability refers to how your child can change to the situation. It is being able to see that something isn't working and to change plans. To be adaptable is to recognize that the blocks keep falling down each time they are all stacked up in one straight line, so something else needs to be changed. Flexibility refers to the ease of which one can be adaptable. It is being able to see that adaptability is needed and to commit without much trouble. Instead of stubbornly continuing to stack blocks and becoming more and more distraught each time they fall, it would be recognizing that maybe they need to have a larger base to provide more stability, and doing so—even if it doesn't match the initial vision for the tower. Resilience is the ability to recover quickly from difficult situations without lasting damage or upset.

All three of these skills are interconnected, yet just different enough to be defined differently. They require being willing to learn and change in order to find better solutions. In a world where we have no idea what is to come, we want our children to learn to become adaptable, flexible, and resilient. In particular, with the 2020 COVID-19 pandemic, many children and adults alike found themselves suddenly needing to cope with the fact that everything was changing. Suddenly, life was no longer the same.

We never know when change is necessary, but being able to deliver it is important. When you are adaptable, flexible, and resilient, you can face the challenges and rise to the occasion. Think about the endless implementations of these skills—maybe your child becomes a surgeon and during surgery, something goes wrong. Someone who isn't adaptable, flexible, and resilient may get so caught up in the emergency and the panic that something is going wrong that they can't change their plan of action to help save the life of the individual. Someone who loses their job may be too distraught to start creating a contingency plan to ensure they don't fall into financial ruin. Some people are more resilient, flexible, and adaptable than others, but even those who struggle with being rigid in their mindsets can begin to develop an acknowledgment and recognition that at the end of the day, they can't control it all.

Within this world, there is only one thing that we can fully control: Ourselves. We can control our reactions to the world around us. We can control how we choose to approach problems. Everything else is out of reach for us; we can't necessarily reach changing other people and how they behave. We can't control the world around us, or the adversities we face. However, in coming to terms with the fact that we can sway how we approach them, we can ensure that we're able to bounce back when we need to.

Raising Adaptable, Flexible, Resilient Children

The best time to start working on resilience is in childhood. Adulthood is full of responsibilities and consequences that aren't necessarily present in a child's life. While a child can do things that have permanent consequences, it is usually our job, as the adults in that child's life, to prevent that. Children essentially live their childhoods in a sort of tutorial for the real world. Not turning in a paper on time may not lead to real, long-term results; but it will lead to a lower grade in a class. Not following the rules at home or in school can lead to being grounded or having detention. Treating other people poorly can lead to losing friends.

There are absolutely consequences in children's lives, but they are much lower-stakes than those we face as adults. Because of this, it's the perfect time to start sowing the seeds of adaptability, flexibility, and resilience. As they face difficult situations, we can guide them through them and gently encourage them to start making any changes that may be necessary along the way.

To develop resilience is to develop the ability to solve problems. It is to develop a way to change behaviors in ways that may be more conducive to success. It gives them the confidence to know that if they need to make a serious change, they can do so successfully. While some children are naturally more inclined toward resilience than others just with personality differences, it is something that can be taught.

Something that all too many parents have forgotten these days is that we don't' exist to coddle our children. Yes, we keep them safe, we love them, and we help them grow, but it isn't our job to protect them from all pain or struggles. In fact, to prevent them from having to face conflict and adversity in childhood when it is relatively low-stakes is to do them a major disservice. Like how children who live in homes that are sanitized constantly and considered very clean are more likely to suffer from allergies, asthma, and hay fever, if we sterilize our children's childhood experiences to avoid all pain and challenges, all we do is stunt their ability to bounce back from them.

Yes, this means that it is *good* for your child to learn how to adapt to struggles. It's *good* to let that toddler continue trying to put up the block tower until he or she finally succeeds on their own. It is beneficial to your teen to struggle with their friend without you and the other parent stepping in to mediate unless there is a real risk of harm. It is good to step back and let your child independently face struggles, with you there on the sidelines and ready to step in if necessary. It's a part of growing up.

That doesn't mean that you play no part in the development of these skills either, however—you play the role of the role model. As you face your own challenges with grace and resilience, your child will pick up on it. Your teen may come to you and ask you about a time where you struggled similarly to get advice from you when they want it; and it's important to share your own experiences when requested. Your children can gain a lot from hearing that you, the adult who has it so easy in their eyes, has struggled as they have. This is beneficial to your child—it shows them that you are present and there for them while still giving them the space and freedom they need to decide when they need the help. By waiting to share until your child is ready, you reinforce the parent-child relationship. You'll also provide them with something real and raw—a moment of weakness.

Of course, this can be difficult for the parent. You want to be there to take away all of the pain. You want to be there to figure out how to protect your child from anything, and that makes sense. But, your desires to assuage your own anxiety and pain do not supercede giving your child or teen the chance to thrive. You find the idea of pain for your child intolerable, so you try to step in and shield them from it themselves, but this is overstepping and will impede on normal development.

When you overstep too much, you essentially teach your child to rely on other people. Your child loses out of the confidence that comes from learning to solve problems on his or her own. They miss out on the ability they have to solve issues on their own because they know that someone else will step in and do it for them. When that doesn't happen, they find themselves completely confused about what to do next. They don't know what to do or who to rely on. As a result, they're stuck.

Children who have problems solved for them aren't prepared to be adults in the real world; they don't know what to do when they're facing adversity or when someone picks on them. They don't know what to do when they're struggling with a job. They may simply give up because there appears to be no other option available to them.

You may have been a helicopter parent, a parent that is constantly hovering over your child or teen to protect them from everything, because you wanted the best for your child. However, the consequences are significant. A child who has been helicopter parents will not be equipped for life alone in adulthood.

Excessive parenting, even when you meant it out of the goodness of your heart, may even lead to an underdevelopment of the brain. Your child's brain develops slowly, not being fully developed until 25 years old. This includes the prefrontal part of the brain, responsible for problem solving.

However, because the brain works by creating and reinforcing neural connections, if you never give your child the chance to practice problem solving, that part of the brain will not develop the same as in a child who has had to make choices on his or her own. You are depriving your child of the chance to exercise the brain and developing a tolerance for failure or challenges, despite the fact that they are a regular part of everyday life.

As a result of stunting the prefrontal cortex, your child may also struggle with emotional self-regulation as well, something that does not work well in adulthood. Children learn to control their emotions through skills that come from experience. If your child has never really dealt with frustration, disappointment, sadness, or other intensely negative emotions, they will grow into an adult that also struggles with coping.

This can also lead to lower self-esteem and confidence. While you may think that protecting your child from negativity will help develop a positive self-image, it actually does the opposite. They believe that they are not trusted to do something right on their own and as a result, they struggle to see themselves as competent.

To raise your child to be adaptable, flexible, and resilient, you have to let them fail sometimes. You have to let them see that sometimes, things go wrong, and that's okay. You need to teach them that they are competent and that they are capable of helping themselves. You can't constantly accommodate each and every want and need they have; they have to learn to cope on their own.

For example, imagine that you have a 5-year-old who is afraid that you will forget her at school. She is terrified of being the last one at the school and cries each day at dropoff because she worries you won't be there to get her. This isn't necessarily an uncommon thought for a new student, especially if she's never gone to preschool or daycare before. Most parents would say that she has to learn to cope with this anxiety and would just show up each day to pick her up when school was over.

However, maybe you think that your child's anxiety is too bad to let her suffer through, so you show up an hour early and pull her out of class, or you park somewhere that your child will be able to see the car from her classroom so she knows you're there significantly earlier and she knows you haven't forgotten her.

This isn't the right solution, either, and if, for whatever reason, you can't be an hour early to pick her up one day, she's going to be terrified you're not coming. This can be incredibly disruptive to her education, and you can't really sit outside of school for an hour each day until she graduates! If you did, you'd spend nearly 2,400 hours just parked outside to assuage her anxiety. Is that really a healthy coping mechanism? Or would your child be better served by learning through experience that you show up each day and learning that her anxiety was unfounded?

This is where learning the right skills comes into play. You can use all sorts of activities that will help your child to understand and cope with the fact that sometimes, things don't work out quite how they thought they would, and that's okay. They can learn that essential emotional self-regulation, and they will start thinking as a problem solver instead of as a victim of circumstance that can't change anything.

Activities to Develop Adaptability, Flexibility, and Resilience in Children

If you want to raise your children or teens to be adaptable, flexible, and resilient, you are doing them a favor that will pay off, especially in adulthood. These skills can be tough and your child may resist the process, especially if you have been there to step in for your children every time in the past. Your children will likely resist being told to think for themselves and solve problems on their own, but in the long run, it will be beneficial to them. As much as it may pain you to see them struggle sometimes, you need to give them the chance to thrive. They will never run if you never let go of their hands when they first learn to walk out of fear of them falling.

Allow Your Child to Fail and Lose

Your child needs to know how to handle failure and losing in life. It can be disappointing, but it is an important life skill that will serve your child well. Have you ever played games with your child and lost on purpose because you didn't want your child to feel bad? Well, now's the time to stop that, especially if it's a game based on luck, such as card and board games. It's understandable to handicap yourself when playing skill-based games, like video games or sports; but for other games where everyone has a fair shot at victory don't always let your child win. Losing will help encourage a development of that emotional self-regulation.

Likewise, you have to also acknowledge to your child that they don't always win. Don't be that parent that shames your child for being on the losing team or for not getting a perfect score on a test. Allow your child to take control of their situation and regulate accordingly. You can be there to commiserate and comfort your child, but you can also remind them that sometimes, we lose, and that's okay.

Let your child work on doing things on his or her own. They may surprise you with how competent they truly are. Remember, you won't be able to follow them around and make sure they do everything just right in adulthood, so don't set that expectation up in childhood.

Change Rules and Routines Sometimes

A good way to encourage your child to learn resilience is to sometimes change things up a bit. While a rigid routine may help you to keep track of everything that you need to get done during the day, it's always a good idea to sometimes ignore the routine altogether and do something else. This creates a tolerance for understanding that you don't have to be perfect. It helps to remind you that there are situations where you won't have everything go the way that you'd expect.

By changing up the routine sometimes, such as deciding to go to a new restaurant, to go and try something new, or deciding to drop everything and go on a hike, you're teaching your child to roll with the punches. Routines have their place, but a child who becomes too accustomed to following an exact routine all the time may struggle when things go awry.

Try Something New Each Day

Each day, make it a point to try something new. Even if that new thing is trying a new food, listening to a new song, or doing something else that you've never done before, you're encouraging an understanding that each day won't be exactly the same. There will always be new things out there. These new things also encourage your child to become tolerant to diversity and differences. Take them to a restaurant that offers a cuisine you've never had before. Go to a different neighborhood in town for a walk. Try a new craft at home. These different tasks help open your mind up to new experiences, which can take your child far as well. Your child will learn to appreciate more and have an open mind, which also lends itself to adaptability and flexibility.

Acknowledging Emotions

When your child or teen is upset, there is no reason that you have to go in and make all of those negative feelings go away. While sometimes a child is just having a bad day and it can be nice to give them a little pick-me-up, that shouldn't be the norm. Acknowledge your child's emotions as they come and name them to your child. For example, if you have a teenager who has been struggling with math and is staring at his homework, completely lost on what to do next, he might snap at you when you ask him to help you set the table for dinner, or if you ask him a simple question. In this situation, it is absolutely appropriate to acknowledge his feelings by name. For example, "I'm sorry you're feeling frustrated with your math homework. However, it's not acceptable for you to take out your frustration on me."

This acknowledgment helps bring awareness to the emotion for your child. This may also help them with acknowledging their emotions more on their own, as well, so they can verbalize how they feel and understand what it is that is bothering them in the moment. This means that they will be able to adapt and adjust their own actions and reactions with their emotional self-awareness, especially as they get older and enter adulthood.

Guide Your Child to the Solution without Giving All of the Answers

While you may feel tempted to swoop in and solve the problems for your child, it is better to guide them to the solution instead. Let's revisit the teen boy frustrated with his homework. Maybe you have a degree in mathematics and you could solve the problem for him in less than a minute. However, to do so would be to hold him back. You won't be there answering the questions on his exams, after all! You won't be there to do his homework in college, either. What you can do, however, is help guide him to the solution instead of just giving him the answer instead. This encourages him to think for himself and figure out how he can solve it instead, while modeling and teaching him how to act.

Similarly, if you have a child who is struggling with her best friend at school, you may stop and consider having a conversation with her about how they have been interacting. You might talk to her about how her friend may be feeling as well in that situation—encouraging your child to think empathetically and come to the right solution instead of simply telling her how to act next time. By guiding your child to the right solution and talking it out with her, she gets exposure to thinking in a more broad situation while also gaining confidence to face those sorts of problems on her own in the future.

Let Your Child Work Through Conflicts

You should also make sure you allow your child to work through conflicts and struggles on his or her own. If there is no danger of harm to anyone or anything, let your child work it out. Give them the chance to make decisions, even if those decisions may be wrong. Now's the time to work on those decision making skills! Conflict is a natural part of life. We won't always agree with each other as we work through life. However, what we can do is recognize that we can learn to disagree in constructive manners. By waiting for your child to fail sometimes, you allow your child to learn important skills and to learn to bounce back after that failure.

Activities to Develop Adaptability, Flexibility, and Resilience in Adults

If you, yourself, struggle with adaptability, flexibility, and resilience, it can be difficult for you to model it for your children. Children look to adults for how they should behave. They look to their parents to learn about their relationships, their conflict solving skills, and other actions. They expect to be able to rely on their parents for guidance, so if you're already struggling to be resilient yourself, your child is going to likely emulate your behaviors as well.

By choosing to take a few steps to build your own tolerance for conflict and struggles, you can help your children to better cope in the future. If you are adaptable with your schedule and how you approach problems, your child will likely pick that up from you. If you bounce back from failure quickly and brush it off as no big deal, your child will likely do the same as well.

If you need some help fostering resilience, adaptability, and flexibility in yourself, try considering many of the points listed above, as well as implementing these activities in your own life:

See the Bigger Picture

When you find yourself frustrated with something, or when things aren't going how you expected, one of the best things that you can do is see the bigger picture in your life. Is what happened really a big deal or can you get past it relatively easily? It's like looking at the child who dropped their ice cream cone and absolutely *loses it* in disappointment. You see it as no big deal and a gross overreaction because you understand that in the grand scheme of things, an ice cream falling is nothing when there are people living on the streets, children starving around the world, and a pandemic that is taking the lives of millions. An ice cream cone? No big deal!

But, can you apply that same principle to yourself and your life? It is worth it to stop and consider the situation around you as well. When something goes wrong, can you stop and put it in context? See the bigger picture. Did you drop your mug and make a big mess when you were trying to get out to work? That's frustrating—but is it really a huge deal in the grand scheme of things? By remembering to stop and consider the bigger picture, you'll be able to feel a bit more resilient. You'll be able to remind yourself that things will be okay and bounce back quicker. It's easier to come up with a game plan when you aren't busy feeling like the world is ending.

Self-Care

Another great way to foster resilience and adaptability is to focus on self-care. This is because when you're stressed out or not in your own peak health, you're going to be quicker to lash out. It's harder to cope with that frustration you may be feeling when you're also worried about other things, short on sleep, or hungry. The better your own physical and mental state is, the easier it is to bounce back from things. You won't think that things going wrong are as bad when you're already in a pretty good position yourself.

Self-care is a broad category for just about anything that you need to take care of yourself. It is to remember to take time for yourself and focus on your own mindset. It is being able to get enough sleep as you need it and to eat and exercise regularly. It is to make sure that your physical and mental needs are met so that you can work on wants or things that you find enjoyment in doing. Without self-care, your body and mind will be under more stress, which are not conducive to these situations.

Change Your Perspective

Finally, you can feel better about the situation that you're in if you can change your perspective. By stopping and considering a situation or conflict, you can start looking at things from other angles. Maybe you're having a fight with your teenager over him keeping his room clean and going to sleep on time each night so he'll be well-rested for school the next day. But, have you ever considered things from his perspective? Science shows us that teenagers tend to have circadian rhythms that keep them awake later at night and encourage them to sleep later in the mornings as well. He may simply not be tired, which is why he's still awake after you've told him to go to sleep, taken his phone and tablet, and threatened to ground him if you caught him awake late.

By stopping and considering things from the perspective of the other person in a conflict, you might start seeing ways that you can change yourself and your behaviors to be more accommodating for the other person without being much of a big deal. Is it really that big of a deal to tell your teenager that if he stays up late, he has to deal with the consequences of being tired all day? He'll self-regulate if you let him. If your preschooler really wants to wear her princess costume to the store, is it really worth the argument to get her to change into something else? She's wearing clothes that are clean and that match already. What's the difference between her costume and a regular dress in her closet? Pick your battles and decide which ones make the most sense for your family. You may be surprised to find that many of the battles you do pick aren't actually worth it.

By stepping back from those battles and changing your own reactions, you're actually able to develop your own resilience. You're able to be more flexible and adaptable as well, and you'll get to reap the benefits for it.

.

Chapter Two: We Are All Works in Progress: The Power of Growth Mindset

As children, it's easy to tell ourselves that we are the best at something. After all, especially as young children, we see the world as primarily those directly around us. You might be the best at math in your classroom, but chances are, there's someone out there in the world who is your age and is even better at math. The same is true in adulthood as well. There are always people out there who are better than we are at things that we may pride ourselves for. This isn't necessarily a bad thing, either—there are just so many people out there in the world that it's hard to pinpoint the best at anything.

When you think that you're the best at something, you may not feel the need to keep practicing. You might be the best employee at your workplace, and as a result, you don't care to build your skills up any further. What you are failing to do, however, is keep up with the fact that even if you are the best at something, perfection is an impossibility. You can always be *better*. There is always room for improvement on just about anything that we do. You could learn to do something quicker. You could learn new skills that will help you in your career line. No matter how good you think you are, you can always do better somewhere.

Unfortunately, people who believe they are the best at something tend to get arrogant. They stop seeing that they could potentially fail at something. They stop acknowledging that they, like all other people, are not infallible. They get so caught up in the idea that they are the best; and they develop excessive confidence that will actually hold them back. Instead of focusing on how they could become *even better,* they are content where they're at.

What these people are missing is a growth mindset. To have a growth mindset is to acknowledge that you are fully capable of improving, no matter how good at something you are. It is to constantly strive for betterment in your life. You're constantly trying to find ways that you can improve. You know that while you might not be able to do something now, that doesn't mean that you can't learn in the future.

In this day and age, things are constantly changing. People are more educated than ever.

Machines are quickly eclipsing many industries that used to be dominated by people. If you let yourself get caught up in the idea that you are good enough, you will never get anywhere else. You'll essentially park yourself in mediocrity, saying that there is no reason to keep moving forward. However, you're not doing yourself any favors by doing so. You need to do more.

Developing a growth mindset is an important skill in this day and age and the sooner that you can develop it, the better you'll do. Children with a growth mindset get that insatiable hunger for improvement and for learning. They yearn for higher achievement. They want to get better endlessly, without seeing a reason to stop. Children in particular also have a natural curiosity to know why things work, how they work, and what could be done to make it better. However, that can quickly be quashed if it isn't fostered. As a parent, it is your job to work on encouraging that mindset that will help your child to succeed. It is your job to foster that desire for further achievement.

What is a Growth Mindset?

Children naturally approach situations differently in their lives. Some children, when met with failure, feel like there's no reason to keep trying. They give up. To some degree, this has to do with resilience. However, it also has to do with mindset as well. We often describe mindsets as either fixed or growth. Some people have a fixed mindset, in which they believe that they are what they are. They believe that they're not good at something and therefore, they'll never be. They don't see a reason to continue trying to better themselves.

Someone with a growth mindset, on the other hand, sees skills as things that can be built up and fostered. They aren't limited to where they are in the moment. They might not be very good at soccer now, but with enough practice, patience, and effort, they can become better. This is why a growth mindset is so important—to have a growth mindset is to recognize that you are full of potential. To teach your child to have a growth mindset is to teach your child that they can always become better than they are in the moment.

That isn't to say that your child isn't "good enough" or that your child should feel bad about where he or she is today. Rather, your child should recognize that they are capable of change if they want it. Your child is capable of learning that new skill, even if it is harder for him than it is for his friend. Your child can grow and adapt, and that can't be discounted.

The Problems with Fixed Mindsets

When people get caught up with a fixed mindset, they assume that skill is innate. They assume that some people are just naturals at what they do. They may look at star athletes and assume that it came naturally to them. They assume that great artists are able to create art without practice. However, this sort of fixed thinking is incredibly limiting. It keeps people from ever trying because they assume that they won't be good enough.

When someone develops a fixed mindset, they assume that failure is absolute. If they fail, it is because they are set to be a failure. They are inadequate; they are incapable of being anything better than that moment of failure. However, we know that this is not the case at all. If your child thinks in this manner, you've probably heard them say, "I'm just no good at this. I'll never be able to do it." They don't believe that they can. They don't feel motivation to learn from their failures and just give in instead of putting in the effort to learn.

For children who develop a fixed mindset, there are three major consequences that cannot be discounted. These three consequences make it difficult for your child to deal with difficulties because they will be quick to simply give in instead of trying harder to get it right in the future.

Decreased Self-Knowledge

The most problematic of the three consequences is decreasing self-knowledge. There is a major emphasis on external rewards as a form of validation instead of focusing on internal development. In other words, your child will believe that the only reason to keep trying to do something or to succeed at anything is because your child wants some sort of extrinsic reward. They want to get a good grade on their test because you'll give them money for every "A" they get. They want to work a job because it will give them money. They want to learn how to paint because they like the attention they get from other people.

However, they don't see things in terms of being happy about the personal development that they'd get, as in learning a new way to do math, or to learn new skills, or to better their ability in painting. They limit their own self-knowledge as a result. They aren't doing anything because they genuinely want to; they just want the end results.

We learn about ourselves through pursuing activities for ourselves. We discover the people that we are inside when we do things for ourselves. A child who draws because they are praised for doing so may not actually enjoy art at all; they just like the praise. They miss out on the chance to find their truest, most authentic selves as a result. As an unintended consequence, they also find that they only find validation from other people instead of getting it where it matters the most: With themselves.

Less Risk-Taking

We live in a world where risks are sometimes necessary. You have to take a risk sometimes if you want to reap rewards. Do you want a job? You risk rejection by applying and putting yourself out there in hopes of getting hired. If you're not willing to take any risks, you'll also struggle to ever reap any rewards.

However, for those with a fixed mindset, it's hard to imagine ever taking any risks at all. They may be so afraid of failure and losing the validation that they're looking for that they don't try at all. They'd rather fail by virtue of not trying at all than to fail by simply lacking the skills. The irony here, however, is that in being inhibited from trying at all, they are failing by default.

The Win at All Costs Mentality

Though many people assume that the world is a dog-eat-dog place where one person's failure guarantees someone else gains something in return, this is not the case. It's easy to think that if you don't get the best result, you lose, especially with a fixed mindset. If you weren't top in your class, then you were a failure. If you didn't get a 100% on a test, you failed. However, all this does is encourage unscrupulous behaviors. If you think that you must get a perfect score or get a job by any means possible, you may find yourself suddenly resorting to all sorts of unhealthy, unfair actions in an attempt to get your way. However, is that really improving yourself the way that you should be?

If your child has this idea that they must always come out on top, are they really getting anywhere at all? Are they really learning what they need, or growing into the person they'd like to be if they deceived people to get there? Athletes may fall for this and choose to take drugs to enhance performance. Businessmen may cheat in order to boost profits. Students may pay someone else to write their papers. However, none of these people are really getting where they'd like to be in a real manner. They are all cheating in hopes of outperforming everyone else. In some times, people may even risk breaking the law in order to succeed.

Now, this doesn't mean that every child with a fixed mindset is poised to become a criminal by any means. However, the mindset can very quickly spiral into one where the ends always justify the means, which is unhealthy. They aren't truly winning anything other than how to cheat the system.

Raising Children with a Growth Mindset

This is where teaching children to have a growth mindset comes into play. Raising children with a growth mindset reminds them that their hard work will be rewarded. It reminds them that if they keep trying, they can succeed. It reminds them that their worth isn't entirely engrossed in how successful they can be or what they do right or wrong.

To raise children with a growth mindset, you need to start off on the right foot by focusing on effort. You want your child to feel supported and loved, without only feeling like they will get praised if they are successful. You want to praise the efforts rather than the end result so your child knows that you are proud of them, even if they're still working on becoming competent.

Praise Effort and Approaches

It's easy to praise your child whenever they succeed. You saw your child trying to do the monkey bars over and over, and when they finally did it, you felt so proud of them! But, by praising the fact that they succeeded, you are putting an unnecessary emphasis on that success rather than the perseverance and resilience to get there.

The best thing that you can do to let your child know that you still love them, even when they fail, is to praise the effort you see them exert. You may say, "Honey, I saw how hard you were trying to get across all those bars. Good job not giving up! Don't you feel so good knowing that you kept trying?" Notice how the praise isn't emphasizing the success—it's emphasizing the perseverance. That lets your child know that you're happy that they kept on trying and also removes the idea that you'll be disappointed if they fail. After all, failure isn't something to be afraid of—it's something to learn from.

Use the Right Language

Growth mindsets are fostered at home, and it begins with you. The way that you speak to your children is the way that they learn to speak to themselves, and because of that, you have a very real obligation to use the right language from the beginning. It can be heartbreaking to hear your child say something like, "I can't do it," when faced with a problem. However, your own language when you speak to your child will shine through and help to provide some degree of guidance that your child can use.

Your own language has to be focused around fostering that growth mindset. When your child says they can't beat the level in their video game, remind them that they can't do it *yet*. With some practice, they will eventually be able to do it, and the fulfillment they'll feel will be absolutely worth it. When your teen comes to you lamenting the fact that they've spent all day studying when they really just wanted to go hang out with friends you can remind them that tomorrow—when they pass their exam—they'll think the effort was worth it.

Avoid limiting language as much as possible, and when you hear those limiting statements coming from your children, such as, "I'm no good. Look at all these mistakes I made!" you can gently remind them that shifting to a growth mindset helps them to feel better and more confident about everything they do. The more that you do this, the easier it becomes for your children to start to emulate it. As they come to recognize that they have the ability to learn and grow as people, they'll learn that the only time they truly fail to do something is when they give up and stop trying. As long as they're still making an effort to do something, it's a work in progress; and they'll reach the end when they reach the end.

Teach Children to Ask for Help

Some children never want to ask for help. To ask for help might be perceived as a sign of weakness. Some might feel discouraged from asking by the people around them, or they're too shy to ask. However, asking for help is a valuable resource. When you're truly stuck on something, being able to ask someone else for their perspective can provide insight and a new perspective to the situation that may reveal a solution. It may also allow for skills to be transferred from someone with experience to someone who is clueless about where to start next.

Never discourage questions, and when you see that your child is stuck, you can ask them if they have any questions about what they're working on. Sometimes, just having someone notice their struggle and asking about it can be enough to encourage them to open up.

Activities to Develop a Growth Mindset in Children

A growth mindset won't build itself, but you can start creating it with several activities that help naturally start to foster such a way of thinking. By engaging with your children in ways that encourage them to understand that they don't have to get things right or be good at something the first time they try something, a growth mindset will set in naturally in ways that are fun and engaging for your children.

Learning about the Brain

Especially if you have younger children who are quick to give up as soon as they try something that doesn't go quite their way, learning about the brain and how skills are built could be a great reminder that most people really *aren't* good at something until they keep trying to build the ability. As children come to learn that the brain is creating new connections during practice, it can become much more exciting and fulfilling to practice.

Imagine your child just tried to do the monkey bars at the playground for the first time and failed. By taking the time to explain that each time that she does something, her brain is creating the connections that will make it easier in the future; you offer her hope that next time, it *will* get easier. It can be exciting to think about the brain making new pathways—it's like exercising your mental muscle instead of your physical ones.

Curiosity

The world around us is so vast that even scientists who have been researching for centuries are still baffled by some of their discoveries. Children tend to come into the world with a natural curiosity about how things work. You might be asked how hummingbirds can flap their wings so quickly or why planes can be in the sky, or why firetrucks are bright red. Children are full of curiosity for the world, but at some point, they may lose interest. They might stop caring about the little details around them, and as they do, they stop working toward learning. The more that your child is exposed to learning, the more likely they are to want to continue learning. The more they are willing to learn, the more likely they are to keep trying after a first effort toward something is fruitless.

"Yet" statements

Any time you catch your child saying that they can't do something, it's a good idea to gently remind them that they can't do it *yet*. "Yet" statements are those that take a negative statement and transform them into a positive observation that can provide further encouragement to keep on trying to do something. Things might be rough now, but if your child starts saying they can't do something *yet*, they're implying that they will be able to do it in the future. That's what matters here; that belief that there is hope in the future for success.

Focusing on the Positive

Part of developing a growth mindset is to be optimistic, both about the future and about oneself. Teaching your child to focus on the positive is one of the best ways that you can prepare your child for life on their own because positivity will take them far. It will remind them to keep trying, or see the bigger picture, and to recognize that even though things are going wrong in the moment, there may be plenty of opportunities to look at things in a positive light. For example, maybe your child dropped their ice cream cone and is heartbroken about it. But, at least it's easy enough to go get a new one to replace it. If her friend doesn't want to play tag with her, she has the opportunity to go make some more friends that will. A teenager who was turned down after asking someone on a date may find someone better in the future. There are so many ways to look at the world in a positive light, and encouraging that optimism begins at home.

Goal Setting

Teaching your child to recognize the importance of setting goals is essential. Sometimes, goals are what keep us moving when we feel like the world is against us. For example, perhaps your teen really wants to pass her driver's exam to get her driver's license before her 17th birthday because she wants to go on a trip with her friend. With that in mind, she prioritizes practicing as much as possible and plans to take her test well before that point. By setting her goal in advance, she also gets the added benefit of being able to retake the exam if necessary later on if she fails the first one. This allows her some degree of flexibility in her goal.

A child who really wants to learn how to draw that cool cartoon character may focus on practicing, little by little, until he completes it. He's got that goal in mind that keeps him practicing, even when the proportions end up a little wonky, or one eye is looking a bit too big compared to the other.

Setting goals gives people something to work toward to continue bettering themselves. It is something that can be used as a sort of motivator that will carry them far. The sooner your children learn to recognize the power of lining up their own goals, the more likely they are to use them to keep them on track and focused on achieving it. They will naturally pick up on the growth mindset as they continue to have something to strive toward.

Activities to Develop a Growth Mindset in Adults

If you never learned to accept a growth mindset in your childhood, you're not out of luck. There are plenty of ways that you can begin developing your own mindset, even now as you work on fostering the growth mindset in your children. Together, you can learn to readjust your perspectives in life to be more positive and beneficial to the two of you.

Accept Imperfection

Perfection isn't accessible for anyone, no matter how hard you may try to be. You might be attempting to be the perfect parent or the perfect partner. However, if you strive for perfection, you're striving for an unattainable goal. You're going to find that it is impossible for you to ever be satisfied with yourself and you may even feel like there's no point in trying because deep down, you *know* you're striving for something unattainable. By accepting imperfection, you recognize that failure isn't the end of the end of the world and is actually something that can provide room for growth.

Find Positives in Failure

Of course, even if you're willing to accept imperfection, you may not be fully tolerant of failure. Failure isn't fun for anyone—it makes you feel like you're not good enough, or like you've disappointed yourself and those around you.

Failure is a valuable learning experience that can help you to grow as a person. When you fail, you may not have achieved your goal, but with failure comes opportunity to grow and do better next time. You learn from your mistakes that were made now so you can do better in the future.

It's much easier to tell our children to do this than it is for us to do it ourselves. We are usually quick to let our children know that their failures are not the end of the world and help them clean up the mess, but for some reason, when we make mistakes, it's much easier to start criticizing ourselves instead of learning.

Learn Something New Each Day

Finally, if you want to really work on that growth mindset, you could make it a point to learn something new each day. By going out of your way to learn one new thing every day, you're naturally creating that better mindset simply because you're actively reminding yourself that there are things you don't know yet. The more you expose yourself to and the more you learn about the world, the more you'll continue striving to grow as a person. You are a work in progress that will always have room for improvement.

Chapter Three: You Deserve to Treat Yourself with Kindness: The Power of Self-Compassion

Have you ever heard a child sadly say that they're no good, not worth the effort, or they're not smart? Hearing a child remark that they're not good enough is heart-wrenching when they're not your children; but if your own child comes to you and voices that they are unhappy with themselves, you may be worried that there's something else going on.

Self-compassion is an essential skill that all people need. Adults and children need it to help themselves feel better in their own minds and bodies. It is known to reduce anxiety and depression, while also being indicative of emotional coping skills. People who lack self-compassion also tend to lack the ability to remind themselves that something going wrong doesn't mean they need to beat themselves up over it. When you've got a child struggling with self-compassion, they may blame themselves and criticize every action and failure they have. They aren't kind to themselves, which of course, continues to tear them down as a person.

While it's often easier to criticize ourselves than to take a compassionate approach, it is also much more harmful. We don't see any reason to continue trying if we're going to beat ourselves up. We might end up getting so caught up in how bad we feel about making a mistake in the past that we don't stop and realize that we can focus on what we'll do next. Instead of being caught up in what you should have done, you can forgive yourself, have compassion to see where your mistakes came from, and then focus on how you can change for next time.

Because children are quick to pick up our own habits, one of the best things that you can do for your children is to show them what self-compassion looks like. It involves being compassionate with yourself while also making sure that you speak to them with compassion as well. The more that you do this, the more they'll absorb. Children are like sponges, and you get to choose what they're exposed to.

What is Self-Compassion?

To have compassion for yourself is essentially the same as having compassion for others, but remembering to apply those same concepts toward yourself as well. When you have compassion for someone else, first you recognize that they are suffering. You see the experience and the pain that it may bring. You must also feel moved by their pain and suffering. The word itself, "compassion," means to "suffer with" someone else. You feel their pain and you want to help. Finally, you realize that suffering is shared—we all feel it.

To be self-compassionate is to recognize that you are struggling. It is to embrace it rather than trying to stuff it away and forget about it. It is to allow yourself to feel your pain that you have and to recognize that you're going through something difficult. No matter what it is that you feel sensitive about, you should be willing to acknowledge it as legitimate. All emotions that we have are valid in their own right, even if not all reactions would be.

Self-compassion reminds you to react toward yourself with the same care that you'd give to your children or loved ones. It is to let go of the judging and criticism so you can be kind toward yourself. You don't do yourself any favors if you criticize yourself for having a hard time. In fact, you may just make those hard feelings even worse.

To have self-compassion is to give way to a healthier mindset. It is to love yourself and recognize that you, like all people, deserve to have those strong negative feelings yourself. You deserve to not be berated for feeling bad about a loss or about not getting something right. To have compassion for yourself is to recognize and acknowledge that you, like everyone else, are human and that you can't be perfect. There is no way for you to ever have that perfection in place.

Dr. Kristin Neff recognizes three key elements of self-compassion that help break it down into something attainable for those who are quick to criticize themselves. Each element is essential to creating that self-compassionate mindset that will help you to understand how you can start embracing your own emotions just as softly and supportively as you would someone else's.

Self-kindness vs. Self-judgment

To have self-compassion is to be understanding in the moment. It is to recognize those feelings of pain, failure, or inadequacy and to allow them to exist. It is to acknowledge them rather than trying to ignore or berate yourself for them. You don't need to punish yourself for feeling bad. It is to acknowledge that you, like everyone else, will fail at some point. You will make mistakes. You will suffer from loss. It is an inevitable part of being human. This recognition of your own suffering must be met with kindness and sympathy.

Common Humanity vs. Isolation

While it can be frustrating for something to go awry, it's also unfair of you to believe that you are the only one who knows your feelings. Every loss, every pain and heartbreak, and every struggle has most likely already been felt by someone else. You are not unique in your suffering. It can feel like it in the moment, but to believe that you are the only one would be naive and irrational. All humans suffer: We love, and we lose. We try and fail sometimes. We make mistakes. However, by recognizing that you are not the only one who suffers, makes mistakes, and fails sometimes, you're able to remind yourself that you are not alone. You step away from the idea of isolation and recognize that you share your imperfections with billions of other people on the planet.

Mindfulness vs. Over-Identification

To be compassionate with yourself is to recognize your emotions and balance them. It is to neither make yourself synonymous with them, nor to suppress them. You must be able to experience and process your emotions and experiences and recognize how they align with those of everyone around you, but also recognize that you cannot let them control you. You need to be able to see and observe your negative emotions and thoughts while reserving judgment that could be harmful or really just serve to make things worse. When you're mindful of your emotions, you recognize the emotions that you have so you *can* be compassionate for them without being caught up in letting your emotions control you.

The Role of Parents in Developing Self-Compassion

When your children come running to you in tears, complaining that they messed up their block tower and they're so bad at building, your first reaction is to soothe them. The block tower might not be important to you, but you can recognize the severity of the situation to your child. Rather than minimizing their very real feelings, you can acknowledge them and see why your child is frustrated. It's easy to have compassion for an upset toddler who spent so long meticulously stacking up all of the blocks, just to accidentally knock them over.

Your voice, reassuring them and acknowledging their emotions, sets the stage for how they'll deal with their pain and upset in the future. By naming their emotions and saying that you can see that they're upset or angry, you're making them feel validated. In the future, they're able to identify and be one with their emotions as well. They will be quicker to recognize their own emotions and see that they're nothing to be ashamed of or bottle up.

Because self-compassion is essential to create self-confidence, this is a crucial foundation for your child to develop. Self-compassion will remind your child that they only need to focus on themselves. They don't need to pay attention to how they compare to other people to be self-compassionate.

Self-compassion can also be beneficial to you as a parent. Because self-compassion will help prevent you from falling victim to self-pity and feeling like a victim, it can help immensely with being able to address many difficult situations— such as being able to keep yourself in control during moments of frustration or when you're struggling with your partner. Especially for new mothers, self-compassion can help alleviate stress.

Of course, our mindsets impact our children as well. If your children see you constantly beating yourself up they're likely to repeat that same behavior. Do you want to see your child tearing themselves down after a mistake? If not, then don't do it to yourself. Treat yourself the way that you want to see your children treat themselves, because they're looking to you for the example of what they should do. They'll repeat what you do.

In fact, a 2015 study from the Behavioural Science Institute in the Netherlands showed that parents who were self-compassionate and avoided self-blame had teens who had fewer struggles and symptoms of both anxiety and depression. They believe that it could be the nonjudgmental self-compassion taught by the parents that allowed the children to feel better about themselves as well.

Granted, self-compassion isn't always easy when you're a parent and have all of that parental guilt hanging over you, but when little eyes are on you, it's important to remember that a little compassion can go a long way. By being self-compassionate, you can be a better parent because you'll feel better and be more capable of dealing with problems as they come along. A major tenet of your ability to have self-compassion will come in the following chapter: mindfulness. As you introduce mindfulness and self-compassion in your life, you can remind yourself that one of the most important things that you can do is forego judgment of yourself. The world will judge you enough without you piling anything else on there as well.

Encouraging Self-Compassion

Your job as the adult in your child's life is to model self-compassion. You can do this by practicing self-compassion out loud. Make sure that you voice your self-compassion out loud. If you have a younger child, you might make a mistake, sigh, and say, "It's okay! Now I know what not to do next time." You might voice your emotions around older children and teenagers in a bit more detail. For example, if you feel frustrated, you could say, "I'm really frustrated because this happened," instead of snapping at others.

To voice your self-compassion to model it for your children is to practice emotional awareness out loud. It is to be capable of putting your emotions in words so they see that you're not bottling them yourself. By vocalizing your emotions, your children see the importance of acknowledging them themselves.

Beyond just modeling self-compassion, you can also guide your child toward it as well. You can remind your child of the importance of being able to acknowledge emotions as they happen so your child feels more comfortable acknowledging them as well. There are plenty of activities that can help children and teens alike in embracing their self-compassion. With that self-compassion they develop, they may feel even more comfortable with themselves. They'll be able to understand that even though they may feel misunderstood, they're not alone.

Activities to Develop Self-Compassion in Children

If you want to start developing self-compassion in your home, one of the best starting points, after modeling self-compassion yourself, is to begin encouraging children to think in ways that will be conducive to that self-compassion later. For example, affirmations are a phenomenal starting point because they remind you to treat yourself with gentle kindness. Some meditations can be designed specifically to aid in self-compassion and self-kindness.

The more that you make self-compassion a priority, the more likely you are to be able to encourage your children to develop these habits as well. It will get easier with time. You'll start automatically being more self-compassionate, and so will your children.

Affirmations

Affirmations are designed to remind you of the changes you need to see in your mindset. They're little statements that are used to ground you and keep your mindset clear so you can maintain control and keep yourself on track toward whatever goals you may have. These are incredibly effective with children as well—an affirmation can help your child to remind themselves of what they need to do when they're angry, or to remind them to quietly remember that they are enough as they are.

Affirmations have three key criteria to be effective: positivity, personal orientation, and in present tense. Each of these three keys will help you to create a solid affirmation that will help you, or your child, remember to take a deep breath and relax. Ideally, affirmations should be positive because it helps create that mind shift. Even when you use statements like "Not scared" or "Not angry," in an affirmation, you're still falling for that same negative, limiting mindset—that is likely to hold you back. A personal affirmation is one that you can influence because you are the subject. You can control whether you love yourself, but you can't control whether someone else loves you. Finally, by keeping your affirmation present-oriented, you remind yourself that the affirmation is true in the moment. You are reminding yourself to make a change to your actions or mindset in that specific moment to be kinder to yourself or to think positively.

For children, the affirmations will probably be simpler than for a teen or an adult. However they are still incredibly useful. For example, if you have a school-aged son who is chronically harsh on himself and regularly voices that he is a failure every time he does less than perfect, you may have him remind himself with the following: "I am trying my hardest and that's what matters." Every time he feels frustrated or like he's doing everything all wrong, he repeats that back to himself. Little by little, it starts happening automatically. He acknowledges that he's trying his hardest and has more compassion for himself when something doesn't work as expected.

For a teen who may think she isn't good enough for her friends or family, you may encourage her to repeat to herself that she is worthy of loving herself and of receiving love from others. This thought process will help her to remind herself that if someone doesn't think she's good enough, then they weren't very good for her anyway.

Other self-compassionate affirmation examples include:

I am worthy of grace.

I am happy to be me.

I deserve to treat myself with kindness and respect.

I'm trying my hardest and that's all I can expect from myself right now.

I'm perfectly imperfect.

I accept who I am, the best and worst parts of me.

It's okay to make mistakes sometimes.

I'm free from self-judgment.

I'm choosing to be kind to myself right now.

I'm choosing to love myself right now.

Positive Letter

This activity is particularly effective for children who can write. Sometimes, older children and teens may find it useful as well. In this activity, your child is tasked with coming up with a letter to themselves. They are to imagine that they are not writing to themselves, but rather, writing to their friend instead, and that their friend is having the same trouble that they were having.

They will likely express that they love their friend, that they respect them for who they are and that they accept their friend for who they are. They should remember that this friend knows everything about them—their positives and negatives. They should write about a moment of compassion for themselves. The letter should be kind and forgiving, acknowledging that it's okay to be sad or feel bad about something while simultaneously choosing not to be mean about it.

This letter, once it is written, should be addressed to your child. They will then read it as if it was intended for them to read, from someone else. The letter should help them to feel better and kinder to themselves, reminding them that they aren't perfect and that they have no obligation to be perfect in the first place.

For example, perhaps your child has been having a hard time with reading at school and she's really hard on herself about it. She feels bad that she's been having a hard time reading, and she judges herself for it harshly—telling herself that she's so stupid or that she's just no good at it, so why bother when she'll never learn to read well? You would then prompt her to stop so she could send a letter to another child who is struggling with soccer, or playing something else she loves and is good at. In this instance, you'd probably have to write the letter to her as she dictated it to you. Her job would be to encourage the other child to keep trying and not to give up because she will learn eventually and that with enough practice, it will get easier. Then, read the letter back to your child, but this time, instead of being addressed to a friend, read it as if it is written to her.

A teen should be able to write and read the letter on his or her own and will be able to use that information for herself. You just have to let them know that you want them to write the letter and leave the rest to them. It should be meaningful and inspire children and teens to recognize that they're kinder to other people than they are to themselves even though really, we should all treat ourselves with tender care and kindness.

Self-Compassion Meditation

Self-compassion can sometimes come in the form of some mindful, reflective meditation. Even young children can be taught and guided through meditation with your help to guide their actions. Older children and teens may appreciate having some scripts played to follow along with. Compassion meditations are among the most common types of meditation and are designed to encourage people to remember their kindness toward themselves. To complete this activity, either provide your older child with the following script, or read it out loud to your younger child.

As you sit down, get comfortable and let your eyes close. Find a good, relaxing place to settle down and think about what you want in your life. What do you want to be? Where do you want to go? How will you get there? Think about this, and breathe deeply.

Repeat the following:

May I be safe.

May I be healthy and strong.

May I be happy with myself and who I am.

May I be at peace.

Think about all of the loving thoughts and feelings you can about yourself. Then, think about someone who helps you to feel good and makes you feel loved. Then repeat the following:

May [name] be safe.

May [name] be healthy and strong.

May [name] be happy with themselves.

May [name] be at peace.

Activities to Develop Self-Compassion in Adults

Adults need self-compassion too. If anything, you're going to need to start with your own self-compassion before you can expect your children to implement it. It can be difficult at first if you've had a lifetime of not keeping these habits, but it's never too late to pick it up. Being able to pick up on how to have your own self-compassion will change your life. It will change how you parent and it will also change how your children choose to act as well.

Practice Self-Care

One of the best ways that you can have self-compassion is through reminding yourself to engage in self-care. Self-care is meeting your needs, both physical and emotional. It is being able to recognize what your needs are and recognizing that you deserve to have them met. Even if it is a few moments of quiet on the deck with a cup of coffee to yourself while the kids play inside, you deserve a moment. You have several needs that need to be met, and while you might feel selfish for doing so, you need to remember that you will be a better parent when you're cared for.

Imagine that you've got a pitcher filled up with water. Throughout the day, you pour the water from your pitcher into everyone else's cup. Pouring into everyone else's cups is how you meet the needs of everyone else. However, what do you do when your pitcher is empty? At some point, you need to fill up, or you're going to run out of water. What are you going to do when you're on empty? Emotionally, you might feel strained and like you're at the end of your rope, and you may even find your emotional restraint is running on low.

You need to take care of yourself if you want to be the best parent you can be, and that means implementing self-care to fill up your own pitcher. Make sure that you're eating and sleeping enough. Get the exercise you need. Find some personal "you" time so you can unwind. The little things can be enough to keep yourself going during the day. Self-compassion and self-care are like two sides of the same coin—they go hand in hand. If you start making it a point to take the time to take care of yourself, you should start feeling better, little by little. You should feel more self-compassionate because you recognize that you need to take care of yourself—emotional needs included.

Reward Yourself

Rewarding your children is usually something that comes naturally—we love treating other people to nice things when it's deserved and acceptable. However, some people really struggle to reward themselves sometimes, too. You deserve to get the occasional reward for your efforts! Parenting is difficult, so you should do something for yourself every now and then as well. A little goes a long way!

When you find yourself getting through a tough week, you might want to consider taking yourself out every now and then for a treat. Let yourself find something that you like. Maybe this looks like having a few days per month where you get to go out and do something kid-free while the other parent takes care of them. Or, perhaps for you, you want that weekly fancy coffee while you do your grocery shopping.

It's easy to tell yourself that you don't deserve the treat when you've had a rough week or when you feel like you're not doing well. You might feel like it's selfish of you to go out and leave the other parent with the kids, or you might think that the money may be spent better if you were to buy something that was necessary instead of what you wanted. Remember this: You deserve to treat yourself! You deserve to feel happy and get a new thing or something that brings you joy every now and then, too.

Make sure that you set out a set time every so often where you do something for you. Make it a part of your routine because you deserve it, and to recognize and acknowledge that you deserve treats and happiness is to practice self-compassion.

How Would You Treat Someone Else?

When you find yourself caught in a funk and criticizing yourself unnecessarily, it's a good time to stop and consider whether that is fair to yourself or not. When you treat yourself harshly, you usually are treating yourself differently than you'd treat other people. It's a good idea to stop and reflect on this from time to time. Let's say you drop a jar at the grocery store and it shatters and sends pickles flying everywhere. You probably feel embarrassed about the mess and the fact that all attention is on you in that moment. It can be humiliating to be stared at, and it would be even worse if you were, for example, to have gotten pickle juice on someone else that was standing near you within the blast zone.

If that happened, you'd probably lash out at yourself. You'd tell yourself that you were so clumsy and stupid. Maybe you told yourself that it's ridiculous that you couldn't even manage to hold a jar right. You may tell yourself that you're useless or worthless. The problem is, you're treating yourself terribly in doing so. You don't deserve that.

If you had just seen someone else drop a jar, what would you think? Chances are, you wouldn't think twice about it and would go right on your way without another thought. If someone else apologized for dropping the same jar and having pickle juice splatter all over your clothes, you'd probably shrug it off, laugh, and let the other person know that it's no big deal and not think twice about it. You might even feel compelled to stop and help the person clean up the mess, while telling them all about the time that you did something similar.

For some reason, we can't keep ourselves from holding ourselves to much harsher standards that we'd hold other people to. We don't like the idea that we made a mistake somewhere along the way. We don't like that we've caused problems. Giving yourself such strict treatment is going to cause you serious problems in life as you continue to criticize every little action.

Self-compassion involves avoiding this by acknowledging the problems that you have and recognizing that we all have them. It is to recognize that we're all that person who dropped something on the ground one time. We've all inconvenienced other people before, and we've all apologized about it. It's important to recognize that you deserve that compassion that you give other people.

Stopping to consider how you consider other people in the same situation as you, reminds you to have some compassion for you as well. You'll see that you're much kinder to other people, though you should always be willing to recognize that you deserve that kindness. We're all human. There's no reason to hold yourself to impossible standards that you'll never be able to meet.

Chapter Four: Living in the Moment: The Power of Mindfulness.

Have you ever found yourself completely immersed in the moment? Maybe it happened when you were listening to a song that you really loved. You just stop and listen closely, hearing each and every note and the rhythm flows through you. You are completely in the moment as you listen to the music and you pay close attention to it. When you are only aware of the music around you, you're in the state of mindfulness.

Mindfulness is a powerful state of mind in which you are completely in the moment, without judgment. You can mindfully eat a meal, or mindfully meditate on your thoughts as they flow. You could mindfully listen to someone else, paying close attention to them and how they present themselves. You can also mindfully reflect on your current moment. To be mindful is to focus on just one thing in the moment. It is to fill your mind with one thing, attending to exactly what you're doing in the present moment.

As simple as this sounds, mindfulness is something that most people don't manage to keep up with something. When you're in the moment, you simply exist without judgment, but most of the time, your mind is on other things. You might be thinking about what you'll do tomorrow or how your meeting went earlier. You lose out on mindfulness without even thinking about it. Your mind starts wandering and suddenly, you find yourself anxious.

Mindfulness is a very important tool in being able to control your emotions; it allows you to understand what you're feeling in the moment, which you can then use to influence how you behave. For example, if you're angry, you can let yourself feel that anger without judging yourself for feeling angry. The awareness of your anger can then help you keep your actions in check. Instead of yelling at someone because you're angry, you can take a deep breath, acknowledge that you feel angry, and move on. There's no need to get upset about how you feel; you just need to move on from it.

Introducing your children to mindfulness is to give them the key to their own minds. It helps them discover their own emotional awareness that they can use to tame their fear of a test they have to take, or to remind them that as heartbroken as they are after their first boyfriend or girlfriend breaks up with them, that things will get better. It reminds them not to take out their frustration from school on their family around them, and to recognize the importance of their own self-care. It is to be able to inspect their own mind so they can see how it is controlling them.

Mindfulness begins at home, and you can introduce it even to young toddlers, with activities to help with calming down and blowing away those strong negative emotions. It may feel unnatural at first, but think about how animals live: in the moment. A dog isn't worried about the past or about the future; it's simply there in the present moment. Now, there's a time and place for planning or thinking about the past, but if you find that you've been dwelling too much on things that you can't really change, are you doing yourself any favors? The past is in the past and there's nothing you can do about what happened before other than recognizing where you could have made improvements. There's no need to let it keep you up at night. If you're struggling with mindfulness now, you might not know what to expect, but rest assured that you and your children can learn it.

What is Mindfulness?

Mindfulness is the ability to be completely and totally present in the moment that we are in. It is to be completely conscious of what you are doing, what's around us, and where we are without being overwhelmed or overreacting to what is around or inside of us. It is to be there to help you to pay attention to the present moment wholly. Every person has the ability to tap into their mindfulness, whether they're aware of it or not. Many young children are experts at it, but as demands in life climb, they lose touch with it.

Think about the last time you saw your child so fully immersed in something that there's nothing you could do to snap them out of it. Maybe they were singing or drawing. Maybe they were playing a game or practicing a sport. Whatever it is, it completely engages them to the point that they're no longer really paying attention to whatever they're *not* doing. For young children, it's usually something to do with make believe or pretend play. They are wholly in the moment, serving their teddies tea from their play kitchen and totally oblivious to what the adults are doing in the next room.

You can tap into that same sort of mindfulness yourself if you train yourself to do so again. It's like riding a bicycle; you might sort of forget it, but as soon as you get back on the seat, you'll be pedaling again in no time. It might be rocky at first, but you'll catch on.

Mindfulness was something that a lot of people disregarded for a very long time, but it's recently gained a sort of resurgence, carried on the wave with yoga and other mindful exercises that are meant to clear the mind and relieve stress. It is commonly associated with meditation, but is not limited to it.

The Parent's Role in Developing Mindful Children

Your role in just about everything in your child's life is essential, but when it comes to mindfulness, remember that without you fostering it, your child is going to struggle to ever build it. Your child is looking to you to model what needs to be done. If you can't implement mindfulness on a regular basis, your child isn't likely to learn it either.

Now, you don't have to take your child off to a meditation retreat or have yoga every morning (but you could!) in order to have a mindful child. These aren't necessary. Sometimes, just a quick mindful hug, lasting just 20 seconds, can be enough to connect with your child and be in the moment. Your child is hardwired for mindfulness, but if you don't continue to encourage it, the mindfulness of childhood is likely to start fading away as life pulls your child in a million different directions.

Mindfulness will start in the home, with mindful exercises every now and then to remind your child how to stick to it. Maybe you go out of your way to eat together, or you spend time reading as a family. We'll be going over several key ways that you can bring mindfulness into the household shortly.

The Benefits of Mindfulness

If you were to search the internet for ways to cope with your stress, anger, lack of self-discipline, or even mental health issues, you'd probably find mindfulness listed as a sort of "cure-all" for everything. It has, admittedly, been overused in many situations, but that does not detract from where it can be one of the most important tools you have! It may not fix all of your problems, but it can be a great solution to many that you may have given up on solving. It can help you calm down when you're angry or regulate your emotions, and so much more. All you have to do is learn to practice it, which we will get to shortly.

Mindfulness is an essential life skill that, once you learn to use properly, may very realistically change your life. From treating depression and anxiety symptoms to healing people to take control of themselves, this is a popular activity that is taught in all sorts of therapeutic settings to help with stress relief. It provides benefits that may surprise you, but you're tapping into a process that will literally help you to rewire your brain.

Reduces Stress

Mindfulness is commonly practiced in order to reduce stress. It works because you're entering a state in which you are simply being. You're not worrying about how you feel or letting it control you; you're just letting the moment pass you by as it is without letting it impact you too strongly. This helps you to reduce your current stress levels in times of concern when you're too stressed out to focus. By practicing mindfulness, you can return yourself to that state of being in control of your emotions enough to reduce your stress.

Beyond that, it helps you with managing future stress as well. You'll be able to calm down your inner mind, which you will probably notice, pretty quickly, can be a crazy place; a place full of constant concerns and stress causing your mind to fly all over the place. With mindfulness, you'll be able to keep your mind clearer.

According to a 2010 analysis by Hoffman et al. it appears that mindfulness-based therapies actually aid in changing the mind. There is an awareness that you develop during regular mindfulness practice that helps you to develop a better stress response to daily triggers.

It Improves Physical Health

We all want to be healthy and raise healthier kids. This is where keeping your physical health up matters immensely. However, it's not always easy to eat right and exercise when you need to. It can be difficult to keep yourself on track and disciplined enough to do the right thing, especially when stress levels start going up and you get busier as you have to shuffle kids from activity to activity, or make sure everyone is ready for school on time.

When you become a more mindful person, however, you're able to help yourself to control your physical health better. You're more likely to manage chronic pain better. This is because our response to pain isn't purely physical—there's a mental aspect to it as well. Especially with chronic pain, you're not only hurting constantly, but also feeling the frustration with it as it happens time and time again. It can be terribly frustrating to feel like you're in pain all the time, but mindfulness can actually help. Higher mindfulness is believed to help lessen pain-related fear, which can also have an effect on the feeling of pain intensity.

Mindfulness can also help with eating better as well. When you're a mindful eater, for example, you can pay attention to your body's hunger cues. This means that you'll only eat what you need. By eating slowly and mindfully, you're reminded to savor food instead of devouring it quickly and risking overeating. This can help you get to the underlying cause of eating too much, such as stress or being an emotional eater.

Boosts Resiliency

When you're mindful, you're usually able to gain a boost to resilience. When you're mindful, you can help yourself cope with negative or difficult emotions better, which you can then regulate more and keep yourself behaving better. You will be able to help yourself overcome those negative thoughts, and by defeating the stress, you may also boost memory and focus.

People who are mindful tend to also be more resilient, which also leads to more lifelong enjoyment over time. When you're mindful, you get to cope better without shutting down, which means you can keep yourself from being too caught up in your emotions and overreacting.

Boosts Relationships

Mindfulness has also been found to be linked to better relationships. Regular mindfulness boosts your own mental health, which also puts you in a better position to cope with your relationships. Relationships of all kinds are all hard; you won't always agree on everything and you'll probably argue with everyone close to you at least every now and then. We aren't able to be perfectly compatible with everyone around us all of the time, and that leads to conflict sometimes.

Because mindfulness brings with it an ability to cope better with stress, it also opens up the ability to better communicate emotions because you'll be more aware of what you're feeling in the moment. You'll be able to tell the other person what you're feeling so they can better understand you. When at least one of the people in the relationship regularly practices mindfulness, there's usually better success in it lasting.

In your own parent-child relationship, you'll likely feel more confident in your own abilities while also boosting your child's social skills. Children will naturally pick up on your mindfulness as you use it and you'll likely implement mindful activities that help to create socially adjusted children who are capable of managing their own emotions and communicating better.

Bringing Mindfulness to the Household

When you bring mindfulness into the home, you'll be benefiting you and your children. It will boost your relationship and also help everyone to be happier and calmer because people are going to be able to cope with their emotions better. Your toddler, who is in full meltdown mode, may calm down if you encourage him to calm down and guide him through a few emotional regulation mindfulness activities. The more he uses them with you, the better he'll get, until one day, you'll hear your child use them on his own without you prompting him.

Your teen may be able to mindfully recognize that her test anxiety is all in her head and recognize that the best thing she can do is calm herself down so she can perform well. After all, if she's stressed out as she goes into the test, she's probably just going to have more troubles with it along the way. She will be too anxious to let herself perform well. The end result is further test anxiety when in reality, a few quick mindfulness exercises could have helped her cope with the feelings.

Modern families seem to be shifting further and further apart, even within the household. There's so much to be done, between work, school, and social lives, that much of the mindfulness that we used to take for granted has started fading away. For example, when's the last time you and your family sat down together and had a proper meal *without any phones or television playing?* This is becoming more of a holiday occurrence that is forgotten about unless it's a special occasion.

Creating a mindful household means that you have to first recognize where you're currently failing to do so. Do you have regular family time that happens without screens or distractions? Are you spending time in the moment, enjoying the closeness that you have with your children? Do you savor their hugs and tell them you love them, looking them in the eyes instead of just saying it as your part? Do you spend time enjoying your family while you're still under one roof? Your children will, one day that will come sooner than you think, fly the nest. By bringing mindfulness back into your home, you'll be able to enjoy it while you still can.

This is something that the whole family is going to have to be on board with. If you're not all willing to spend the time together and play by all the rules, you're going to have a hard time implementing them. You may even realize that you actually were missing out on these moments as you start implementing them. You will bond as a family as you continue to connect together. Your children will benefit from this sense of identity gained from your family.

Children who have a sense of familial identity, who spend regular time with their whole families, tend to do better in peer pressure situations. They recognize the values that they have and that were instilled by their family and are more likely to stick to them. They're likely to perform better in school and in their social life, and all you have to do to bring these benefits into your home is to start implementing mindfulness. Make your home a mindful one. You don't have to spend every moment together, but you can make the moments that you do spend together mindful. Try considering these different additions to your family routine to see how they influence your life together.

Sharing Highs and Lows Each Day

Every day, preferably over dinner, spend some time talking about the highs and lows of your day. Everyone should absolutely share without trying to come up with noncommittal answers like "all of it was good," or "I had no lows." This is a great way to introduce your children to the idea of thinking about how they felt all day while also helping them to see that everyone, including Mom and Dad, have their struggles. Life isn't always easy for anyone, but children tend to forget that sometimes, even their parents don't have it good. Sure, you can do whatever you want when you're an adult, but that comes with all sorts of important responsibilities, like paying bills and making sure the kids are all taken care of as well. It can be stressful sometimes.

This will help you understand how your child is doing as well. You'll be spending more time talking with them, which can be crucial when your children get to be school age and beyond. When you start spending much less time with them while they go off and do their own things or spend time with their friends more than they spend at home.

Spend Time Reading Together

Reading is an act of mindfulness in and of itself—you are usually totally immersed in the book you're reading without really paying attention to the outside world. It is also a great way to wind down at the end of the night after spending a day busy and running around. Make reading part of your family tradition—turn off the electronics an hour before bed and spend some of that time together as a family, reading. Young children can be read to, while older children may enjoy sharing a book together as well and then talking about it afterward. You get the physical closeness of everyone together, the focus on the story, and you even have some new conversation material to enjoy as well.

Go Hiking Together

Hiking may not be for everyone, but it is a great way to get out of the house and enjoy the nature around you. If you live close to some nice hiking trails, consider enjoying them as a family. If not, you could probably find a local park where you can spend some time out in nature. Even a nightly walk through the neighborhood can be a great way to get yourself up on your feet, moving around, and enjoying time together.

The key here, however, is to use your walk as a point of mindfulness. Take the time to be quiet as you walk, listening to the sounds around you. Watch the grass dancing in the wind, or the shadows stretching across the pavement. As you pay attention to these different parts of the world around you, you'll be immersed in the moment, practicing mindfulness. When you're done with your walk, take some time to talk about what was found. You might have seen different things than your children did, or they may have noticed something you didn't.

Create Family Traditions

Every family should have some sort of tradition they always do. Whether it's baking, playing games, going out dancing, hiking, or anything else, try to foster a love for something that everyone in the family shares. This will help you to foster that family identity. If possible, make sure this happens on a regular basis and, ideally, it'd be something that you could do without electronics or getting other people involved—so you can really be fully present in the moment.

Let Your Kids Have a Voice

Children often get the impression that their thoughts don't matter. They may ask you for something or say that they want to do something, only to be shot down immediately. They might ask for a toy they want, just to be told no, or they may ask to go to that party down the street where you know no parents will be home, and you tell them it's not happening. Children of all ages, from toddlers to teenagers know the frustration of being told that they don't get a say in something. However, this doesn't really prepare them to start making their own decisions either.

Whenever appropriate, make sure that your children get a chance to voice their opinions. This is a practice in mindfulness in its own right—your children are learning to express their thoughts and feelings in a clear, cohesive manner so they get to make a decision. While you may not always say yes to what they've asked for, at least they've had a chance to explain where they were coming for. This can help them to learn to stand up for themselves and to feel like it's okay for them to express their own opinions without fear of always being told no.

Activities to Develop Mindfulness in Children

To bring mindfulness directly to your child, there are all sorts of different activities that you can start using. These activities can be great ways to help your child develop the understanding of mindfulness so they can tap into it as necessary. For example, take the mindful breathing exercise. This one can be made very accessible for young children, and you can use it as a way to cue to your children to calm down. The next time you're at the grocery store with a toddler screaming for a piece of candy, you'd be able to walk them through how to calm themselves down, and that skill will last a lifetime. An older child who may struggle with anxiety will be able to remind themselves that the anxiety isn't necessarily controlling their life and that they can make a decision to tame it themselves.

Mindfulness Grounding Activity

To ground yourself is to bring yourself back to the present moment. We all face times when our emotions completely overwhelm us. It can be hard for us to feel like we can control ourselves through our anger or frustration, so we turn to mindfulness to help with that. For young children, it gets even harder. A toddler or child isn't going to be able to cope with their anger the same way an adult can. Their brains are still developing and that means that they have a harder time with emotional regulation. However, they can still learn it, and the sooner they do, the more ingrained it can become.

This exercise is quite simple to use—to use it, you will encourage your child to engage with all senses in a time of emotional crisis. When your child is so overcome with emotion that you feel like there's no talking through it, you can bring them down to earth, so to speak with this exercise. For example, say you have a young child who is sleeping away from home for the first time in a hotel. Maybe he's scared of the strange sounds and sights in the room. Maybe there are louder planes and louder traffic there than in his room. Maybe he's not used to hearing people walking above him. If he's crying in fear, you might have a hard time calming him down. However, a grounding exercise can help bring him back.

Start by talking about five things seen around you. These can be anything—just make sure that you describe them in great detail. Perhaps you see one blinking light from the smoke alarm, a curtain blowing with the fan, the white blanket on the bed, the silly fruit bowl painting on the wall, and your child's favorite plushie on his tummy.

Then, move on to four things that can be heard. Surely, there are many different sounds if he's scared of the room, right? Talk about the sound of the plane overhead, and the whir of the fan. You can hear big brother snoring in the other bed, and the sound of the water in the pipes.

Third is three things that you can feel around you, focusing on the texture. Maybe the blanket is a sort of scratchy cotton feeling. The plushie on his stomach is soft and fluffy. The feeling of your hand is warm and soft.

Fourth, identify two things you can smell around you. Maybe you smell the bleach used to clean the sheets before putting them on the bed, and the smell of the pizza you ate for a late dinner when you got to your room.

Finally, identify one feeling. This could be fear of being somewhere new, or it could be sadness because he's not in his bed at ohme.

By the time you count down through all five senses, your child should be feeling calmer and more in control of themselves. This means that you're probably more satisfied with a quieter, happier child as well and everyone can enjoy that good night's rest. An older child could use this as a way to come down from anger or anxiety as well, simply going through the list mentally without needing help from a parent.

Mindful Breathing

To breathe mindfully is to focus entirely on the breaths that you take, focusing on the sensations as you do. It is a powerful tool in calming down from strong emotions because as you breathe deeply, you trigger your heart rate to slow down automatically. As you start making those physical changes to your body, your mental state starts to change as well—leaving you feeling better.

This is quite simple—encourage your child to close his or her eyes, then count breaths together. You want to count breaths in equal spaces.

Younger children are probably comfortable with three-second breaths while older ones and adults may be able to do four-second breaths more comfortably. You will want to breathe in, hold, and breathe out for equal counts.

Encourage your child to stop and take a deep breath in as you count. Then, your child should hold the breath for a count, followed by exhaling the breath for the same count, and finally, holding their breath again. For example:

Breathe in slowly for three seconds

Hold the breath for three seconds

Breathe out slowly for three seconds

Wait three seconds to breathe in again

This should be repeated for a few minutes for the best effect. Usually, it only takes a few breaths before the effect takes hold. Inhales should be through the nose while exhales should always pass through the mouth.

For very young children who have a hard time with deep breathing, you could even consider having them lying on their backs with a favorite toy on their tummies so their breath moves the toy up and down; and they can get some real visual feedback as they go.

Mindful Nature Walk

Taking a mindful walk through nature is a great family-oriented activity that can really help you and your family connect while recharging in the great outdoors. Find a park or trail that you can all enjoy, then take the time to walk through it together. You don't have to rush, and you should be comfortable just mindfully meandering down the trail. Let your child set the pace as you go. If they see something that catches their eye, stop and investigate it. It's all about taking the time to get to know the world around you without feeling rushed or like you have to get somewhere quickly. You want to make sure that you're able to take the time to really enjoy the world around you. When you see things from your child's perspective, you may notice something new, too. You may not have thought to flip over that rock, but your child did, and there was a cool salamander under it.

As you walk, talk about what you see and what you feel. The walk doesn't have to be silent if you don't want it to be. Your child will likely want to talk all about the various things you see and seeing the world through their eyes can actually be a great reminder to you about mindfulness as well. You'll both gain something out of this adventure together and you'll be able to talk to each other about it. You may even choose to make this a hobby that you enjoy together.

Mindful Chime

Have you ever heard those chimes that, once rung, seem to echo for what feels like forever, slowly reverberating through the air and fading out of existence? These beautiful sounds can actually be used as a mindfulness tool. When you ring them and let them ring around you, focusing only on the sound for as long as it exists, you can practice that extended mindfulness. These chimes are commonly used in yoga and mediation for this very purpose. All you need to do is give a quick tap of the chime, then listen to the sound until it naturally fades out on its own.

Your children may get enjoyment out of taking turns to ring the chime as well, bringing a further sense of happiness to the process. You can use just about any chime that's meant to last, or a singing bowl.

Activities to Develop Mindfulness in Adults

For adults, learning mindfulness isn't much different than in children. the only difference is that many exercises tend to assume that you're much more patient or you don't need the implementation of a game or task to practice it. Of course, any of the previously mentioned activities will work just fine for you as an adult as well. However, if you prefer a more refined activity that will keep you focused more on mindfulness and meditation, you may prefer to use meditation, breathing exercises, or yoga to your advantage.

Meditation

Meditation is perhaps the classic activity that people think of when they hear the world mindfulness. Though mindfulness doesn't have to be through meditation, it is an effective way to trigger it. One of the best mindfulness meditations to use is a body scan. These simple meditations help you to slowly, body part by body part, go over your body to see how you're feeling. The more you practice this, the easier it will get; but you should catch on pretty quickly with this simple exercise.

To begin, find somewhere nice and comfortable, where you won't be distracted. You can choose where, so long as it's quiet. Your pose also isn't important, so long as you won't feel the need to move around too much as you go. Perhaps you consider laying in your bed. Once you're in position, close your eyes and breathe deeply. You should take a few deep breaths, focusing on the sensation of the air flowing through your body. Then, once you start feeling relaxed, focus on the tip of your toes. Notice any sensations you have in them. Are they tense? If so, relax them. Then, move to your feet. Again, entice the sensations and release any tension.

You'll repeat this process, slowly extending up the body to understand how you're feeling. You don't have to rush it—you should do it thoroughly. Move from your feet to your calves, then thighs. Move on to your pelvis, then lower stomach. Focus on your back, and on your chest. Analyze your shoulders, followed by your arms, then hands. Feel your neck, your face, and finally, the top of your head.

This process should allow you to slowly but thoroughly feel any sensations that you have, and you'll be able to hear the thoughts you have as well. You'll be able to recognize how you're feeling better so you'll be able to move on. the more that you focus on yourself like this, the more mindfulness you'll develop.

Breathing Exercises

When you feel something negative and feel like you might overreact, it's perfectly acceptable to implement a breathing exercise to help rein in the emotions. Just mindfully breathing deeply, in and out, can be a huge mood changer when you're stressed or upset about something. It helps you to ground yourself, while also triggering the calming effect of your breathing.

Yoga

Yoga is another one of those activities that a lot of people may turn down, but it can help a lot with mindfulness. As you perform each pose, the emphasis is on breathing deeply and feeling the pose in your own body. Many people love to use this before they start meditating, letting themselves enjoy the benefits of calming down before shifting gears into meditation.

Because yoga is meant to be a sort of connection between body and mind, allowing you to achieve a calm, enjoyable life, it also fosters mindfulness. It is a way to foster awareness, which is exactly what mindfulness entails. Typically, you'll use several poses and breathing, all of which helps you to ensure that you're able to focus on your body. You feel the stretching of your body, recognizing that any tightness that you feel is only temporary and will pass soon.

You can find countless videos online for free with guides on yoga routines, or you can choose to join local classes. When you gain competence in the motions that you use, you may even choose to create your own routines instead. Some of the most common beginner's poses include:

Corpse Pose

This may not sound like the most pleasant of poses for relaxation, but is a common one used as a beginning and ending pose. To begin, rest on your back, feet spread shoulder-width apart. Let your arms rest at your sides, palms up. Go completely limp and relax without resistance. As you do, let yourself breathe deeply. Don't try to control it. Just pay attention to the way that you breathe in and out.

Eye of the Needle Pose

From the Corpse pose, move your feet to the floor, pulling them in toward your bottom, now hip-width apart. Then, let your right shin rest on your left thigh, bringing your left knee inward to touch your chest. Then, push your right arm through the gap between your legs and wrap your left arm around the outside, bringing your hands together and intertwining your fingers. How is your breathing feeling? Focus on your breathing and any stretching that you feel in your hips. Don't change anything about the pose—just enjoy the moment for a few deep breaths until you feel ready to release it.

Cat-Cow Pose

Move now to your hands and knees, with your hands squarely underneath your shoulders and your knees and hips aligned. Breathe deeply, and as you breathe out, let your back round out, pulling your tailbone between your legs. Let your head fall naturally, tilting so you can see your thighs. As you breathe in, tilt the pelvis back inward instead, bending your back gently. Stretch your head up, raising your crown without lifting your chin too high. Move back and forth as you breathe for a few rounds, focusing on the sensations.

Downward Dog

Transition to this pose from the Cat-Cow Pose. Start by moving your toes down to the ground, then raising your hips up and letting your legs straighten out. Your bottom is now pointed up in the air, like a dog in a play bow. Stay there, feeling the stretch and breathe 10 to 20 times in this position.

Mountain Pose

The Mountain pose is commonly thought of as being inactive, but it is actually a foundation for just about any standing pose you may choose. Begin while standing, arms left to dangle at your sides. Plant your feet into the ground, shifting your weight until it is even, then center it so all weight is on your heels. Straighten your back without bending it, relaxing your shoulders and keeping your chin parallel to the ground. Stand there and be present in the feelings you notice. What do you feel? How is your mind? Breathe here for a few breaths.

Chapter Five: We All Have Inner Artists: The Power of Creativity.

Children are born with a natural propensity for creativity. They may see a stick on the ground and see a grand sword to slay the dragon, or they have a stone that becomes a magical gem that powers their spaceship as they travel across the galaxies. They might see a few bits of trash and think to themselves that they can make a great project out of it, and often, they do it. Children are born wanting to create. They see potential where we see garbage. They see whimsical games and create riveting tales in their minds as they play, tapping into an imagination that we can only marvel at as adults.

Even Picasso recognized this, famously stating, "Every child is an artist. The problem is how to remain an artist once we grow up." He isn't wrong. How often are children criticized for wanting to pursue art in life? Maybe your child is enamored with art, drawing constantly, and when he gets older, he tells you that his life goal is to be a video game graphic artist. He loves it so much that he wants to spend his whole life doing it. You might look at his art, likely unrefined still in the early days, and tell him that it's a pipe dream and that he needs to let it go because art doesn't pay the bills.

Maybe your daughter came to you, shyly admitting that what she wants more than anything is to be a singer. You might laugh and tell her that almost no one makes money as a singer and that she still needs to go to college "just in case." What do you think this does to your child's self-esteem or to their desire to continue creating?

Adults in the world tend to look at creative outlets as fun hobbies, but not as options for actual careers. Yet, adults also spend money on video games, to stream movies and television that has been scripted by artists and acted by artists, and listen to music performed by artists as they drive to work. They eat food packaged in boxes designed by artists, and probably read a book written by an artist. To create a piece of art is to create an intensely personal part of oneself and share it with the world. If you, their parent who is supposed to be their number-one fan, tells them to knock it off and get real, what do you think they're going to think?

Creativity will be quelled, they will let it go, and end up letting their artistic talents go untamed.

No 13-year-old who wants to be a graphic designer has to be a perfect artist—school is there to help get the techniques needed later on. However, you can interfere immediately by telling your child not to bother. You may as well tell him to get in the mold and to conform to the rest of society.

Children are creative naturally, but that creativity can be dampened by adults who criticize and judge them for it. These days, children steadily lose their propensity for creativity as they age—each year they're in school, they get a little bit further away from it until suddenly, they stop drawing, painting, singing, or writing forever.

You don't have to do anything to build creativity—all you have to do is let it happen and support your child when they come to you to show them that intimate piece of themselves that they created in the real world. They took something that was from within them to share with you, and that deserves respect and acknowledgment.

Creativity isn't just about art, either. There are so many different ways that creativity alters the way that we think and how we go about the world. For example, creativity influences how we solve problems. Someone who is creative may see a solution to a problem that you never thought to think of. Someone creative may come up with a fantastic business model that they only felt brave enough to put out because they believed in themselves. Someone had to be creative enough to think that each and every technological advancement we've made would be possible. For example, if you were to go back 200 years, the idea that we'd have cars that run without a horse pulling a cart would seem fantastical at best. However, as new technology is created, the potential for novel solutions to problems arises. This is how we move toward the future. Perhaps your child will have some mind-blowing realization about cancer as an adult and discover the cure for it! It will be their creativity, problem-solving, and ingenuity that generates that new way of thinking. Our future problems will be solved by creating new solutions to them. Technology advances to become more streamlined, but that is only possible if we, the people, come up with new solutions.

Creativity starts within children, but you have a duty as their parent to help foster it so they continue to remember and act upon it as they grow. Your job is to let them continue to be creative so that creativity can continue to grow and flourish within them. They will do all of the watering needed to plant the seed as long as you keep external obstacles from blocking the sunlight.

The Importance of Creativity

Creativity is so much more than just coloring pictures to put on the fridge. It involves freeing your ideas to let them flow, allowing for more learning and creative solutions to problems. It allows for the world to grow and change with innovative ideas that sprout. Creativity is for all people, and it is actually beneficial beyond what we'd normally think.

Creativity Creates Confidence

Sharing art isn't always easy. Especially for people who are especially shy, it can be something that they really don't take lightly. A teenager may be hesitant about showing you the story they wrote, or your child might be afraid you won't like the drawing they made for you. Especially if they've faced criticism in the past, sharing art may not come easily to your children. However, to be creative allows your child to continue to grow. Slowly, confidence can build as skills are also developed.

Your child may come to realize that he can write a great story that his friends thought was great, and that goes a long way in boosting his confidence. A teen may realize that she's actually got great talent on a guitar and go on to start a band that plays in a talent show for the school. You never know what a child will become, and whether they become an artist or not, confidence is necessary. Why not let children build it in a fun manner?

Creativity Solves Problems

When you're faced with a problem, you're probably worried about figuring out how to solve it. Children think this way as well. We've all seen pictures of those creative kids on the internet that found a way to shirk around the intent of a rule to get their way while still following the guidelines set out for them. One such example is a child told that they cannot eat in the living room, but cannot have the tablet in the kitchen. The child sat at the dividing line between the tile and carpet, with the tablet on the carpet and with him on the tile. He ate his snack while not being in the living room, and still got to enjoy his tablet.

That is creativity and ingenuity at its finest. Children who are creative often see solutions we'd never dream of. Did that parent expect their child to find a way to break the rule without actually breaking the rule? Probably not—but can the child really be blamed for trying? Fostering this kind of creativity is what your child needs in order to thrive, and in doing so, you can create a critical thinker who will be ready to take on anything the world throws their way.

Creativity Nourishes the Brain

Because creativity encourages you to use your brain more often, you usually see more connections built. As you use your brain, your brain creates new pathways for each skill. Those pathways are expanded and grown upon the more you build your skills. Art engages the whole mind and can actually keep your brain healthier. Creative people also tend to see stressors differently—they are able to overcome struggles rather than being stressed out by them.

Creativity and Problem-Solving

You might not think that creativity would be important in most jobs, but the truth is, finding the creative answer can actually be one of the best skills to have in many jobs. Entrepreneurs are a major proponent of this—they solve problems with the businesses or products they advertise. While creativity is not the only factor that goes into problem solving, it can be one of the most influential.

When you're creative, you start coming up with new ways of thinking that others may not consider. This means that in problem solving, you're more likely to come up with a good solution that can help the entire team. Problem solving is influenced by creativity in several ways, such as in creating new strategies, breaking barriers, and finding the optimal solution.

Creating New Strategies with Creativity

Whether in a business or a classroom, or even in a conflict between friends, being able to discover a new strategy that will help with solving the problem is essential. Maybe you and your partner always argue about the same thing and neither party is willing to budge—a creative person may come up with some solution that helps eliminate the issue. Maybe your children are arguing with each other about which movie the family is going to watch. You might be able to come up with some creative strategy to break the tie without either child feeling like they were slighted.

Creativity allows for thinking outside the box. You might consider playing a game for the deciding vote, or you may create a schedule that allows everyone to rotate choosing the movie. If you have a child that doesn't respond well to most traditional disciplines, you come up with a strategy that works well for them. Maybe a toddler who doesn't like listening is won over by creating a street light with red, yellow, and green lights for behavior. Red light may be for when the child is at his or her emotional limit and needs a positive time out to let their biggest emotions pass and to sort of reset before rejoining the group, while yellow serves as a warning, and green determines that the child is on good behavior.

These are creative solutions for parents. In the instance of children, it could be sitting on that line with the tablet during a snack without breaking rules, or maybe your child comes up with a new game to solve their boredom. There are so many different ways that your child can be creative, and as they strategize new ways, they're likely to build confidence along the way.

Breaking Barriers with Creativity

Our children and teens are constantly inundated with barriers that restrict them needlessly. They might be told that they can never be a game engineer because they're a girl and girls can't be gamers. Maybe they're told that they can't go to college because they're poor, or they don't deserve to be on the sports team because of their body type. Barriers may also follow into adulthood, with stereotypes being unfairly applied in many situations.

Children who are creative tend to have a much better time being able to come up with solutions. They're more likely to find the way that they can and will be able to get past any of their barriers they face. Maybe they come up with something that allows them to excel. Maybe they allow their creativity to keep them striving for better and they even discover, eventually, that there are ways they can keep trying to break free from any barriers that they face. The more that they work toward bettering themselves, the more likely they are to start seeing how they can succeed. They'll take the barriers and find new ways over, under, around, and through them. They will have the tenacity to keep striving for a solution to their problem—they just have to find it.

Finding the Optimal Solution with Creativity

When you raise creative children, they turn into adults who can see the ways that they need to act if they want to make changes. When they have a problem, they understand that they have to be able to find the best solution to it. They develop the ability to be able to see multiple solutions and start to recognize which is likely to be the right one. They may even start taking parts of several solutions and putting them together in hopes of being able to create the best one. Creativity helps them to think about things that might not otherwise cross their minds.

Entrepreneurship and Creativity

Every leader needs to be creative to some degree. Entrepreneurs need to be even more so if they want to succeed. It's rare that people see entrepreneurs for their problem-solving, but rather, how they present their ideas. Typically, people expect entrepreneurs to be highly creative, however creativity may also be seen in a negative, almost chaotic light. You may expect someone to, for example, be uninhibited due to their creativity, which may be seen as a detriment to their abilities to succeed at just about anything. After all, to be entrepreneurial, you have to have a sort of leadership mindset. However, creativity and leadership don't appear to go hand in hand when leaders are supposed to be practical and calm to maintain control. Control and creativity almost appear to be two conflicting personality types to many people. This is a major misconception, however—your creativity isn't necessarily a sign of how in control you are.

Rather, creativity is about being able to think outside of constraints. It may very well still be under control and manageable, at which point, creativity may be a huge benefit. Think about the last time creativity helped you with something. Did you come up with an innovative solution to a problem you had? Did you find a way to make something work when you thought you couldn't? Did you create something new? Creativity is about making something new—even if that new thing is a solution to a problem.

To be creative is known to be linked to all sorts of positive benefits in children and adults. When you raise your children while fostering that degree of creativity, you'll be able to find ways that you can better yourself. You'll find several benefits that will lend themselves directly to being entrepreneurial.

Better Success Rates

Intelligence matters in life when trying to become successful in careers, but there's more to it than just that. You may be highly intelligent, but if you're not creative enough to use that intelligence for more and to ensure that you use it effectively, then you're going to be letting it go to waste. Aspiring entrepreneurs require creativity in their lives and careers just as much as they need their intelligence, and even more in some situations.

Unfortunately, however, there is a huge emphasis on intelligence and rote memorization than there is on creative thinking. Schools tend to test on the ability to simply memorize things, but the problem is that memorization doesn't create the creativity that is necessary for entrepreneurs to identify a problem and a solution to that problem that isn't already out there for them. They need to have the ability to show themselves as capable. Creativity in employees and entrepreneurs can be a game changer when the skills are used adequately, and it's a skill that will definitely be required for the future.

Better Productivity

Better productivity is often fostered through creativity because individuals are able to explore uncharted territories, so to speak, with the desire to discover new solutions. As you allow yourself to develop the ability to explore problems that others may be too afraid to touch, you foster your own productivity further because you keep yourself motivated. You also may need less time trying to solve problems because you were able to start exploring them from different angles right off the bat.

Critical Thinking

As your children develop the ability to become more creative and learn to foster and harness it, they can also become much better at critical thinking. Problems are often solved with creativity, and that works best when the creativity is honed through the use of critical thinking. Essentially, creativity allows for entrepreneurs to think both in convergent or divergent thinking.

Convergent thinking refers to in-depth analysis of something to find the best solution possible in a situation. It lets people start using data and hard numbers to come up with solutions to measurable problems. Divergent thinking, on the other hand, allows for creativity by exploring all sorts of different solutions to the same problems. When both convergent and divergent thinking are combined, the best solutions are likely to be found.

Raising Creative Children

With all of these benefits, it comes as no surprise that so many people are trying to raise creative children these days. When you want to foster creativity in your children, one of the best things that you can do is remember that you simply need to allow the inner creativity your children already have to continue to grow over time. It doesn't take much—just stay out of their way and let their creativity spread.

Creativity is our most free form of self-expression—it is fulfilling to take how we feel or what we think and put it into a form that can be shared with others. Children love the ability to do so. They love being able to express themselves completely without judgment, and if you can prevent any sort of judgment from going their way, you set them up with the tools they'll need. Then, the rest is up to them!

If you're concerned about unintentionally inhibiting creativity, there are several actions that you can take to influence your parenting that should help to ensure that your children do get to explore their truest parts of themselves and learn to express themselves creatively.

No Idea is a Bad Idea

Your children's minds are full of ideas. From seeing a cardboard toilet paper roll and seeing the potential for it to become a cool new toy, to being able to see things from perspectives that they haven't yet been taught to ignore, your children naturally come up with their own ideas. Their ideas themselves are their own manifestations of creativity in their own rights. Being able to foster creativity is as simple as letting ideas continue.

Most people would balk at the phrase, "No idea is a bad idea." After all, things are bound to be inherently bad, right? Well, the trick here is letting your children work that out for themselves. Don't make them afraid to think by criticizing their ideas. Imagine that your young child has asked you, "When you were a kid, was everything *really* in black and white?" Maybe the only exposure to older media that your child has is in black and white and they naturally think that the whole world must have been like that.

Is that right? Not at all—but your child is thinking critically and creatively, and that deserves praise on its own. Instead of making your child feel bad about themselves, maybe you should discuss their reasoning for why they think that. You don't have to tell them that they're right to acknowledge that they had a good way of thinking before correcting them. A simple, "Wow, that makes a lot of sense! I can see why you think that way, but really, we had color. We just didn't have cameras that could record color yet," would go a long way.

Instead of laughing at your child for making that connection, you show that you're happy to listen to what your child thinks. Your child is then less likely to fear making mistakes. As they don't fear mistakes or being wrong about something they thought they understood, they're more likely to continue thinking creatively. Those who are afraid of making mistakes may feel like they're better off not trying to think creatively. As a result, they start losing touch with that ability to think in creative manners.

Avoid Labels

It can be easy to label your children as they're younger. You might tell them that they're so creative, or they're so smart, or they're better at something else. However, there's a problem with this: The labels you create for your children become the boxes they use to limit themselves. You might be trying to validate them at something, but by labeling them, you're really just making them believe that they have to identify with that thing.

Instead, it's always better to label the action. By labeling the action rather than the child, you don't limit them. Instead of saying, "You're so smart!" you could say, "Wow, that's a good thought!" As you allow those labels to be presented to your child, there's a much better chance that your child is going to catch onto them. As they box themselves in, they also start discouraging themselves. If you've told them that they're much better at math than writing, you will put it in their heads that it's not a good idea to practice writing because they're not good at it anyway.

Avoiding the labels helps you to assist your children in exploring several different subjects equally instead of feeling pressured into pursuing something in particular based upon judgments passed by other people. This is even true in the teens—your teen might hear you say, "Wow, you're much better at your science class than your English class," and that could really hinder their passions. Maybe your child is an aspiring author, but you didn't know that and you just told them that they're not very good at writing. Do you think your teen is really going to want to continue pursuing something their parents told them they weren't good at?

Supporting Passions

Of course, not every child is going to like every little thing. This is to be expected and you don't need to push them to do it all or to love it all. There's no sense in telling your child that they need to really like to draw when they prefer singing. What you can do instead is to support their passions. You want your children to feel confident about what they're doing on their own and they will naturally pursue their own passions. What you can do is support their passions, no matter what they are.

In younger children, this is all about spotting what they seem to gravitate toward and then encourage it. You might notice that your children really like to draw, so you encourage them to draw by providing them plenty of crafts that they can use. An older child who is passionate about music may ask to be put into music lessons to get better, and you can do that as a way of supporting their passions. Your teen may want certain art supplies or a tablet to practice art on. Or, perhaps you have a child passionate about playing sports or dancing. No matter what it is, the best thing you can do is to support what they love without judgment.

This also means that if they eventually decide to quit what they're doing, you need to avoid judgment. It takes time for children to discover what they're passionate about and that means that you need to let them experiment with themselves as much as possible. They'll find it eventually.

Limit Screen Time

For the most part, screen time can be an active detriment to creativity, especially if it involves passively watching a movie or television show. As you watch TV, you generally absorb information without really processing it much. When you spend hours on the television, then, you're missing out on hours that could have gone toward creative thinking.

This is especially true for children. Instead of mindless absorption of television, encourage them to do something more creative. Maybe you have them play games, or have them create digital art or write. It's not necessarily the screens that inhibit creativity when there are plenty of ways that you can be creative with screens anyway. From composing music to writing, or even coding new video games, screens can be essential mediums for art. However, the creative benefits only apply if your child is actively creating instead of, for example, binge watching movies.

Provide the Supplies

Whatever your child is interested in doing, it's generally a good idea to provide them with the necessary supplies. Creativity is a trait that goes far in life, so fostering it as much as possible by providing the creative mediums for your child to engage in them is highly beneficial. You want to make sure that you make it a point to show your children that creativity can be fun. Make sure the supplies vary as well. Perhaps you have 2D and 3D mediums for your younger children, or you provide programs for an older child or teen to create art on a tablet or computer

Activities to Develop Creativity in Children

When you want to foster creativity and creative thoughts, there are many ways that you can implement them regularly. From simply talking about creative things to engaging in roleplay, you can foster that creative part of the mind. There are so many different points in the day that you can use for developing creativity, especially because you don't have to do anything but use your mind and your voice. That means that time spent driving, which many parents do with their children more than they'd like to anyway as children get shuttled around, can then become great opportunities to foster these creative thoughts.

Roleplaying

Roleplaying is a fancy word for playing pretend. When you roleplay, you take the role of someone else in order to go through a different situation. You can use this for all sorts of creative thinking activities because you can take an infinite number of roles. Now, you could sit down and play a role playing game with older children if that's your cup of tea—they're fantastic for boosting creative thoughts. However, you can also simply pose small scenarios where you have to act them out.

For younger children, for example, you could come up with a scenario where you're stuck in a tree and can't get down, and the child has to help you. They don't have a ladder. What are they going to do? Your child would then have to think critically about how they could possibly get you out of the tree. It could be great fun!

For older children, you can raise the stakes: "You're going to the movies when suddenly, your favorite movie star pops out! What do you do?" You can have all sorts of relevant prompts that allow for a degree of creativity while also being engaging to children of all ages.

A Day without Toys

If you have younger children, you may have a few too many toys sitting around, gathering dust. However, your child really doesn't need many toys in the first place. To emphasize this, spend a day without any toys at all. Your child will be tasked with spending the whole day without getting to touch any toys. They'll probably go out of their way to find ways to play with other things or to craft or pretend that the stick they find is their sword while they go play.

For older children, you can emulate this by having a day without electronics. Your teen may not be very happy about it, but this can be a great way to force them to go out of their way to do something else that would be more productive.

Fun Hypothetical Questions

A fun game to play in the car involves taking turns asking the most ridiculous hypothetical questions that everyone can come up with, then hearing the answers that people have. Have you ever wondered what your teen would do in a massive zombie apocalypse? Or how your child would react if they were woken up by a unicorn that wanted to go on a magic adventure?

These hypothetical questions can be as bizarre and open ended as you want to make them. The fun is in hearing all of the random answers that you have to pass on to them. For example, what if you're wondering what your child would do if they were on the beach when a giant narwhal came flying through the sky to tell them that the world was in danger and only they could save it?

Suddenly, you've given what is essentially a prompt for a whole book. In fact, you might even inspire your child to write that story later after having to brainstorm and explain to you what they'd do. By encouraging those creative thoughts, you also encourage other creative activities, such as writing stories in this manner.

Activities to Develop Creativity in Adults

Of course, if you're not exactly primed for creativity yourself, then you might be somewhat doubtful about being able to encourage your children. No matter how old you are, you'll see serious benefits to being able to become a more creative individual. The more creative you are as an individual, the more likely you are to develop the benefits that we've already discussed. You'll also likely find that being able to support your children in their creative endeavors will help you as well.

Collaborations

One of the best ways to develop creativity is to collaborate with other people. When you're collaborating, whether at work or on a personal project, you have to work around someone else.

You can't just take full control of something and assume it'll be just fine. You have to make sure you're seeing the other person's input, choices, and their actions as well. This works because creativity doesn't exactly exist in a vacuum— sometimes, just working with someone else is enough to help you to see new perspectives that you can use to change how you were planning on succeeding.

When you work with other people, you may take ideas from watching their own attempts or solutions to success. You may be able to, for example, see how someone else chooses to paint a picture, and you draw inspiration from it. Collaborating with other people allows you to gain that inspiration and to start using it to your advantage as much as possible.

Do Something You Love with a Twist

Another way you can start building your own creativity is to do something you love, but do it differently. If you love to paint, for example, maybe you try your hand at diamond painting. Or, if you love to write poetry, maybe you choose to write a small story. Doing something you love but with a twist is a great way to get your mind working in new ways. It helps to create new neural pathways in your brain that can build upon the old ones. You're doing something that is similar to something that you already know how to do; it might not seem nearly as intimidating.

Make Something

Of course, creativity all boils down to creating something, whether that something is a new solution to a problem, a new story, art, or anything else. Even baking and cooking is an art form in its own right. Taking the time to make something new always engages with the creative part of your brain. It doesn't matter what you choose to make—just make *something.* Try to do so regularly for the best benefits.

Chapter Six: We Have One Planet: The Power of Sustainability

We have just one planet that we live on. That one planet has a very delicate ecosystem, which we are a part of. Everything that we do directly interacts with the planet, and we are very quickly reaching a point of no return in which the planet will be damaged beyond what we can really repair given current technological limitations. Our planet matters immensely, and while for so long, people took the stance of the people of tomorrow can fix the problem, there's a major issue there: The people of tomorrow are our children and grandchildren.

Do we really want to leave our children worse off than we were? Do we really want to make them solve problems that we caused because we were too lazy or uncommitted to fix them ourselves? Do we really want our children to inherit a dying planet because we couldn't be bothered to make relatively small changes in our daily routines? As the parents and grandparents of the generation of tomorrow, we owe the children better. We owe them a planet that they can trust to take care of them, as when the planet is depleted, there is nowhere else to turn. There is no planet B where they can go to take care of their needs.

Now, we might not have all the right answers to live a clean life, but we do have the resources to start changing the trajectory we're heading on. We might not be able to completely eliminate human waste now, but we can start making changes that will help buy more time until we *do* know how to eliminate the waste. This is where sustainability comes into play.

What is Sustainability?

Sustainability is the idea that something can be maintained. In terms of the planet, it is to avoid depleting any natural resources to ensure that the future generation has the same amount, or more, or a resource than we do, rather than depleting what they'll have. To live sustainably, we must be able to meet our own needs without compromising the needs of the next generations. There are only so many resources out there; we only have so much space and time that can be used. Likewise, there is only so much damage and abuse the planet can take, between pollution and depletion before it will no longer be able to sustain life.

Our planet is unique in the sense that it is *perfect* for life. It's not too far away from the sun, nor is it too close. It has just the right combination of elements that come together to create water and other elements of life. It has the perfect atmosphere that it uses to prevent damage from the sun's harmful rays. The chances of finding another planet that is as suitable for life as ours is incredibly slim, so we owe it to ourselves and humanity's future to practice sustainable habits that will ensure that generations to come don't have to contend with our problems.

These days, sustainability is often synonymous with environmentally friendly. According to the UCLA Sustainability Committee, sustainability can be defined as a way to integrate environmental health, economic viability, and social equity to enable communities for now and for the future that are resilient, healthy, thriving, and diverse. Essentially, it recognizes how the world is interconnected, and it acknowledges that, in order to be environmentally healthy, something has to protect the health and vitality of not just people, but also the ecology and economy. In a world with finite resources, they should all be used in ways that will allow for long-term growth. We all want what's best for our children, and what they need is a world that can continue to sustain them.

To leave behind a world that is uninhabitable, or is going to cause problems with our children accessing essentials, such as food or water, we are doing them a disservice. We are setting them up for failure by expecting them to survive in a world that we've destroyed. If they can't grow food, what are they going to do? People will starve. If they don't have access to clean air or water, people will become ill and possibly even die.

Sustainability doesn't mean foregoing all grocery shopping and instead growing all of your food, or choosing to buy an electric vehicle and go entirely waste-free. This isn't actually financially feasible for most people, but you can make some choices and changes to your family's household that can help change the trajectory toward a more sustainable way of living. You can choose to recycle and compost, or to cut out plastic shopping bags that are increasingly becoming less and less common. You can choose to avoid purchasing products in reusable bags, and also make it a point to repair and reuse various household wares and goods around your home. These changes might not seem like much, but each year, you can lessen and prevent some of the damage to the environment. If everyone pitches in together, the difference will be noticeable for all.

The Importance of Sustainability

Now, you might think that sustainability doesn't matter so much on the individual level; we all need to make the necessary changes if we want to leave behind a world that our children and grandchildren can enjoy. From what you eat and wear to how you choose to brush your teeth and shower, you can make an impact on the world that can very quickly start to add up. When's the last time you thought about how often you drive? Or how you bring your groceries home from the store? These different actions all create different impacts on the environment.

Sustainability matters because without it, irreparable harm will be done to the environment. Greenhouse gas emissions are driven up by food consumption, especially when you don't make it a point to eat sustainably. For example, maybe you don't make it a point to buy locally and to eat lower on the food chain. How far did that tomato on your plate have to travel in order to get to you? How much waste was created by the beef in your burger? What about the cheese and the lettuce? When everything has to be outsourced and brought from elsewhere in the country, or even the world, suddenly you're contributing to the transportation costs as well.

Scientists agree that we're teetering on the edge of ecological disaster, but that we can make significant changes if we know what we're doing. You can cut your household's carbon footprint, which can help you to contribute to being a part of the solution. Typically, waste goes up depending on wealth. Wealthier individuals, despite having the means to cut their carbon footprints, tend to use and produce *more* waste rather than less, and that waste sits around, polluting the environment. They fill up landfills, enjoy food that may have had to be imported from further away to get what they wanted, and often buy more than people who are not as wealthy. They may choose to throw away things that break instead of repurposing or repairing them because they don't think it's worth the time or effort. As a result, objects that probably could have been repaired wind up in landfills.

The pollution of the world is the product of every single person in the world to varying degrees. It will take a massive shift to make a difference and change how our world is run and therefore, the health of our ecology. However, to believe that because you are just one cog on the environmental scale and therefore your choices don't matter is wrong. To think that you don't need to teach your children to worry about or take care of the environment is to take what we have for granted. However, the past shows that taking clean air and water for granted creates more pollution. You need to be able to see how your changes that you make will impact not just you and your family, but the whole world.

The Role of Parents in Encouraging Sustainability

By creating the rules of your household and setting the pace for expectations, you're responsible for encouraging sustainability. You can teach your children to have an innate care for their environments so they, to, choose to take care of it. It's not just for social brownie points—your planet and the planet for the people of tomorrow need you to take care of it.

Your choices and actions will be followed by your children. They'll see that you make it a point to grab a canvas bag before shopping to prevent yourself from being a part of the problem. Sure, that's just one more plastic bag out of the landfills, but when it takes a single plastic bag more than 500 or more years to decompose, at which point it has simply degraded into a more toxic pollutant, that one bag makes a difference. The more bags you forego over your lifetime, you forego hundreds of years of pollution.

When you consider that the average American family uses nearly 1,500 plastic bags per year and only 1% of those bags are recycled, you can see that the amount of pollution adds up rapidly. Before you know it, that plastic sits around, far outlasting the people who used them for all of 12 minutes. Making a choice to use reusable bags as a family will rub off on your children. They'll recognize that you're making these changes, and especially if you talk to them, they are likely to follow along. Teaching them to have respect and love for their world begins at home.

Simple Steps toward a Sustainable Household

Thankfully, not all aspects of creating a more sustainable home have to feel excessive or like they're difficult. While there is often a bit more effort and sometimes a bit more cost in making the sustainable choice, the benefits are well worth it. By beginning at home, you'll be able to prevent some waste from polluting the world.

However, if you want a real impact, the best thing you can do is ensure that you make it a household affair. Everyone needs to pitch in and do their part to reduce the footprint your family has on the world. The more that people choose to make the pledge to do so, the healthier the planet has the chance to become.

If you're ready to start making the changes that need to be seen in the world but don't know where to start, thankfully there are a few intuitive places where you can begin. Some small changes can create lifelong habits that will then help to reduce pollution. If we all made these changes, the planet would be so much healthier!

Recycling

One of the most obvious ways that you can protect the environment is to recycle as much as possible. It is becoming increasingly more common for recycling to no longer be seen as a luxury to be paid for on the garbage bill, but rather as a way that you can help contribute to sustainability. Many companies will even incentivise people to recycle by providing bins up to a certain size for free, or as a credit on the bill.

Recycling is incredibly easy, with the rules varying from community to community. Some allow for everything to be placed in one container while others may require several different bins for the various recyclables you have. You can teach your children to recycle by asking them to contribute. Teach younger children about why it matters and get them involved. Encourage them to sort and rinse items as they use them. Teach them how to place their waste in the right bin for recyclables and encourage them to get involved with taking the recycling to the curb or bringing it back into the house.

Composting

Food waste makes up a major portion of what gets thrown out each year. From eggshells to coffee grounds and even your grass clippings, you need to consider how much waste you'd add to your local landfills if you threw everything away. While food waste and yard trimmings are compostable and they will break down relatively quickly compared to everything else in the dump, they'll also cause it to fill up prematurely.

By composting your food waste at home, you'll be able to keep critical food waste out of the dumps, which is essential when you consider that 1 ton of organic waste being removed from a dump would be the equivalent of removing a car from the road for two whole months. It might not sound impressive at first, but when you consider that in the US alone, there are 40 million tons of food wasted each year. That means that by composting, a massive amount of food waste can be diverted, which is highly beneficial to the environment over time.

As an added benefit, when you compost your food waste, you also get to use the resulting material as fertilizer for your soil. When you garden, you probably need to buy fertilizer if you want to have food produced, and that may mean even more packaging when you buy it commercially. Or, you can skip the middleman altogether and make your own.

Reusable Bags

Plastic bags wreak havoc on the world around us. The average plastic bag is used for just 12 minutes at a time—the amount of time it takes for people to take their purchases home. Those bags then sit around, eventually get thrown out, and then rot in landfills for upwards of 500 years. This amount of pollution can wreak havoc on the world, especially as plastic starts spilling into the ocean.

Did you know that 1 in 3 leatherback sea turtles have been found to have plastic in their stomachs? By choosing to avoid plastic bags as much as you can, you help to reduce the carbon footprint you leave on the planet. Even paper bags are better, as they can be recycled or composted. Ideally, however, you'd choose to get your own reusable bags to use whenever you shop.

Choosing Green Products

So many commercial products aren't exactly kind to the environment. Many of them can create plenty of pollutants just to produce them. Others may be toxic to the environment. Most of the time, when it's time to clean, you can turn to simple household items that can be used to clean, disinfect, and deodorize messes without nearly as much pollution involved. What this means for you is that you can choose safer alternatives to many household chemicals. You could use vinegar and baking soda to clean many different surfaces without needing to use bleach.

Avoid Single-Serve Packages

While it could be convenient to rely on single-serve packaging when you're busy each day with putting your children's lunches together, or when you're busy and on the go, single-serve packages add a significant amount of waste. This waste can very easily be cut down simply by making it a point to buy products that your family enjoys in bulk and then provide reusable containers that your child can then fill up and bring home with the desired amount of what they want. It takes a little bit more effort, but it goes a long way in keeping trash out of landfills.

Repair and Repurpose

When something breaks, is your first instinct to throw it away? Many people think that once something is no longer good for its original purpose, it belongs in the garbage. While some things may not have much reusability potential, there are many objects that very well could be reused in other ways. For example, perhaps you have a big bath towel that your dog chewed a hole in. You might think that it's best to throw it away and move on. However, that bath towel could actually be cut up and used as cleaning rags, which would also reduce the amount of paper towels that your family would use. Or, perhaps you have a chair that had a leg break. You could repair the leg, or you could throw it out and buy a new chair. Many people prefer to replace the chair altogether because they think it's easier. However, it's also more wasteful, especially if the repairs are not serious. Making it a point to repair broken items before throwing them away, or repurposing them when you can't repair them can be a great way to keep items out of landfills.

Meatless Days

While meat may taste good, it also isn't sustainable to eat regularly, especially if you choose to buy commercial meat that requires valuable resources to transport from the farm to your table. By choosing to eat meat less often and to enjoy fruits and vegetables more, you'll reduce the carbon footprint you put on the world. By buying sustainable, organic, local produce when you can, you're able to cut down on toxins and transportation costs.

This doesn't mean that you need to go vegan—but you can cut out the meat and dairy you enjoy a few times per week. Maybe implement meatless Mondays into your household routine and maybe enjoy vegetarian lunches on occasion. These little choices go a long way.

Saving Water

Water is used heavily each day by every person. Whether you're actively consuming it, using it to shower, flushing toilets, or using it to cook or clean, people use a massive amount of water. The food that you consume needs water to grow as well, and the food your food consumes, in the instances of meat, also need water to grow. That's a whole lot of water!

While you still need to drink water, shower, and use the toilet, you can start cutting down on how much water you use daily and influence how your children use the water as well. For example, try implementing the following:

- Turning water off when not rinsing off toothbrush while brushing teeth instead of letting it run
- Limit showers and use water-saving showerheads
- Only run dishwasher and washing machines when they're full loads
- Wash produce in a bowl of clean water
- Keep water in the refrigerator rather than running the tap until it's cold
- Water your lawn sparingly, and when you do water it, do so early morning and deep soak the lawn.

Packing Lunch

While it can be nice to go out for lunch each day, it's really unsustainable to buy something packaged every day. Not only are you contributing to waste, you're also going to be spending a lot of money to do so. It can help to pack lunch each day, prioritizing using reusable containers and silverware rather than one-time-use disposable options that may be convenient, but are harmful to the environment.

Activities to Develop Sustainability in Children

If your children are interested in learning to be sustainable, there are many ways they can help to protect the planet. We all have a responsibility to do our part and that means being able to teach your children how they can be more sustainable in their day to day lives. There are several activities that you can encourage your children to do to introduce them to sustainability in a positive light. As your child commits to these different actions, they'll start to develop their own newfound respect for nature around them.

Reuse Items for Crafts

One thing that can help children not only think creatively, but also develop a sustainable mindset is to recognize that they can use items for crafts along the way. Consider saving everyday items and encouraging your children to think about them. Maybe you keep tabs from soda cans or cardboard boxes from your deliveries so your child can find something fun to do with them. Children are masters of creating what they need to play when they're given the supplies to do so, so if you want to see your children enjoying themselves while also helping to reduce the amount of waste in the world, you can do so by taking the time to reuse items. The more times you've used something, the better. In giving your children things that they can use to craft, you actually encourage them to stop and consider how they can use the resources at their disposal as well.

Create a Vegetable Garden

Gardening teaches children several important lessons, and when you focus on growing fruits and veggies instead of growing pretty flowers, you put your resources and water into creating food that will be enjoyable and beneficial. Plus, when you grow your food at home, you cut down on the transportation costs to get something for yourself. Being able to grow your one food also teaches children where their food comes from.

Growing a garden also creates a special relationship between people and the environment around them. They get to see first hand how their actions will directly impact how the plants grow. They'll also get the added benefit of being able to take care of their own gardens. This gives them a newfound respect for the world around them as they see how truly delicate the ecosystem can be.

Even if you don't have a lot of space outside or if you live in an apartment, you can still grow some vegetables and herbs in your home. Many plants grow just fine in planters and containers if you want to grow a tomato plant on your deck, or if you want a little basket of strawberries. Or, if you don't have any outside space at all, consider growing a garden indoors, using herbs or greens. There are many different options—you'll just have to look into what you can grow in your area.

Play Outside

Like creating a garden for your children, you should encourage your children to play outside because it helps them to connect with nature.

Children who play outside regularly get the added benefit of taking the time out of their day to go out and enjoy nature. They enjoy being among the trees and smelling flowers or hearing the birds singing. All of this is only possible so long as the world around us is taken care of.

The more that your child enjoys being in nature, the more likely they are to try to protect it as well. They'll have a vested interest in being able to continue enjoying nature as they can, and that means they're more likely to do what they can. They're more likely to want to protect what they love. They'll feel like it's important for them to choose how they can be sustainable themselves so they don't hurt the world they've come to love.

Make Homemade Paper

What better way to teach children about recycling than to help them to make their own paper? You'll get to teach your child all about how paper is processed and made, and they'll have fun while they're at it. Making paper at home is actually far easier than most people seem to believe. It just takes some patience and a willingness to learn. To do this, you will need:

- Paper scraps

- Containers to soak paper
- Cookie cutters (if you want to shape your paper)
- Frame with fine mesh screen
- Container to catch water
- Old blender
- Felt
- Newspaper

When you're ready to get started, you'll need to commit to a couple days of time. Do the following:

1. Take your paper and tear it up into pieces the size of a coin. You can use one color, many colors, or white paper you dye with food coloring.
2. Take containers that you'll use to soak your paper and fill them up halfway with water. Then, fill it up with paper scraps. Generally, you'll want to sort out colors that aren't too similar, or you'll end up with a brown, mushy mess.
3. Let the paper soak up the water for at least 24 hours.
4. After the paper has soaked overnight, add about half a cup of paper to the blender with a cup of additional water. If you want

to add glitter or colors, do so now. Then, process the paper until it breaks into a pulp.

5. Take your frame screen and place it across a big container that will take water. Then, put your cookie cutter on top to shape the paper (or you can skip this if you want freeform shapes).

6. Pour the pulp into the cookie cutter, or pour it directly onto the screen in the general shape you're going for.

7. Leave the paper to drip freely for five minutes, then use your fingers to gently push down on the pump to force out more of the water.

8. Remove the cookie cutter at this point if you've used one, while still leaving the paper on the screen. Put your felt over the top and press it into the screen to soak up extra moisture.

9. Lift the paper off from the screen gently and let it dry on the newspaper.

If you wanted to be really creative and emphasize growing plants, you could even mix some seeds into the pulp after you've blended it. The seeds can then germinate over time and be planted right into your garden.

Activities to Develop Sustainability in Adults

If you've never really fostered your own desire to be more sustainable, now's a great time to start. Your own love for the environment will be what grows on your child. Your children will see your actions and choose to mimic them. Your children will pick up on your respect for the environment and to care for the world around you if they see you doing it first.

Bike, Walk, or Ride Public Transportation to Work

By walking, biking, or riding public transportation to work where you can, you help cut down on the pollution created by driving to and from work. Plus, if you walk or bike, you get the added benefit of enjoying the time out in nature, and also getting your exercise in! If you can't make any of those options, carpooling to and from work is another great way to get another car off the road while still getting to work.

Donation Day

In order to further emphasize your ability to think sustainably, consider making it a point to go through your home and purge out things that you no longer need. Whether they're clothes that have been outgrown or you no longer enjoy wearing, all the old baby supplies that you don't use, or books that haven't been opened in years, you can gather up your belongings and clear them out.

Donating your old belongings that are in good condition helps you to keep things out of landfills because other people can meet their needs without buying new products and you don't throw anything away. Essentially, you lessen waste because your items provide a solution to a need for several people instead of just one. Most items can be purchased secondhand without much of a concern.

When you finish purging your belongings and donating what is still in good condition, you can then start considering the uses for other objects as well. If they're broken, can they be reasonably repaired? If not, can you use them for something else? A cracked jug may not hold water very well anymore, but it could make a nice planter to save yourself the cost of getting a new one and to prevent it from going to get processed through recycling before its time.

Make Your Own Soap

You may be surprised to know that, most of the time, the suds in the soaps you use are really just to make you feel like they've got strong cleaning power. Soap could foam less and still work effectively. Many businesses encourage you to use more soap than you actually need when cleaning because they want you to buy more soap. The more you use, the more soap you buy, and the more soap you buy, the more money lines their pockets.

Whether you choose to make laundry soap, dishwasher detergent combinations, or hand soap, you've got options that will help you to clean what needs to be cleaned, while paying less and protecting the environment.

For example, imagine that you're going to do laundry with your own soap blend. Instead of buying a big jug of liquid detergent, you can mix your own. While you will need to buy more supplies, you'll be able to make more. By combining hot water, a grated bar of soap, borax, washing soda, and essential oils, you'll make your own liquid detergent that can save you money and also help the environment as well.

Chapter Seven: A Little Thankfulness Goes a Long Way: The Power Of Gratitude

When's the last time you said thank you to the people around you? Have you said thank you to your children after they've done something you requested? When have you thought to yourself that you have enough of something instead of looking to what you can get next? All too often, we run into this feeling of unhappiness because we're constantly comparing ourselves to other people. We all end up telling ourselves that we'll get happier when we get to the next level.

Maybe you've been trying to save up for your vacation to travel somewhere you've always wanted to go, but the entire time you're on vacation, you find yourself wishing that you had the money to do it better. Instead of being thankful you're on vacation with your family, you tell yourself that next time, you want to rent the suite at the hotel instead of just a room with a couple of beds. Instead of telling yourself that you're lucky you got tickets to that show you went to, you think about how much better it would have been to get front row tickets. The entire time, you're so preoccupied with the fact that you weren't able to get the best that you forget to enjoy the moment.

When you forget your gratitude, you wind up keeping yourself down. You lose sight of the present moment because you don't have something better, but the problem is that someone always has something better. When you really just want better just to have it, you forget that you have more than most other people do. You're lucky to be happy and healthy. You're lucky to have opportunities afforded to you. You're lucky to be able to support your family.

We're quick to call our children out when they behave ungratefully, but when we don't lead by example, we really just make the problem worse. They're going to follow your lead and if you're constantly wanting something better, why wouldn't your children also want better? The result is unhappiness on all sides.

What is Gratitude?

Gratitude is the act of recognizing that you have something that is worth appreciating. When you're grateful about what you have, you recognize that the good in your life deserves appreciation. By appreciating the good things, you're able to get past the bad so much easier. The bad doesn't seem as overwhelming when you've got the good reminding you not to sweat it. For example, imagine that you didn't get a promotion at work— at least you still have a job! To be grateful for your job doesn't mean you're happy that you didn't get the promotion, it just means that you recognize what you still have.

Now, imagine that you just bought your teenager a brand new phone. Instead of getting them a top of the line iPhone, you get them something that costs half the price, but still works well. Most children would probably be pleased to get something like that, but your teen may decide that they're unsatisfied. They might yell and complain and say that it's unfair that they have to use some generic phone while all their friends have iPhones.

Whether you can afford the iPhone or not, you don't owe your child a top of the line phone. You actually don't owe them a phone at all. You could have chosen to tell your child to get a job to earn it instead of providing it for them. After the blatant lack of gratitude, you may choose to do just that. It's clear that your child missed the gratitude memo and therefore doesn't actually need to have the phone you gave them. Of course, you'll probably have more of a fight on your hands afterward, but a little gratitude goes a long way.

To have gratitude is to appreciate what you have and to recognize that you don't have to have it. It is to recognize that you're not entitled to what you have, and that you're lucky to have what you do. We may express our gratitude through saying a simple "thank you" after someone does something for us, or we may feel thankful and appreciative when we receive something from someone else, whether it is time, energy, or emotional labor. You can appreciate someone being willing to sit and speak to you, or you can appreciate when your good friends help you to achieve a goal. You can appreciate the effort your parents put into raising you, or the effort that you've put into getting your job.

Gratitude is an emotion that shows our own recognition of what other people have done for us and what we've received in return for our own efforts. You didn't necessarily have to go on vacation, but you were lucky enough to be able to afford it, even if it wasn't a first-class experience. Your child didn't necessarily need a phone, but you chose to do the nice thing and provide one for them.

Gratitude is essential—it shows other people that you acknowledge and appreciate what they've done for you. Even if it's as simple as holding the door open for you while you're juggling several bags, other people have chosen to help and acknowledge you. They've chosen to make your life easier in some way and that is what matters. Your gratitude shows that you are appreciative of their efforts.

Gratitude and Positivity

As you cultivate gratitude, you create positivity. Instead of focusing on what you don't have, you focus on what you do. This is an essential lesson, especially for children and teens who may not recognize that they're lucky to have what they do have. The world can be unfair, and it may not be fair that your child doesn't get a brand new convertible right after getting their license when someone else in the class may.

The world isn't fair and you aren't owed anything. The same sentiment extends to your children as well; they can't expect to be given everything they want in the world. It'd be unrealistic for them to expect to get everything handed to them on a silver platter, despite that being what so many children assume they deserve when they grow up without any gratitude.

However, with gratitude, the inherent unfairness of the world doesn't seem too bad because instead of looking at what you don't have, you see that you're incredibly lucky to have what you *do* have. You recognize that what you do have is worthy of your appreciation and you do what you can to acknowledge that.

Gratitude is known to create positivity. When you're grateful for what you have, you're more likely to be happier and positive in general. You'll feel more satisfied in life, knowing that you have more than you're guaranteed, and you feel less materialistic as a result. Your gratitude for what you have and the positive attitude you develop then goes on to create a wide range of positive benefits to your health as well. You're more likely to be healthier and less fatigued because you don't constantly stress yourself out about what other people have and what you don't.

It also improves prosocial behaviors because you're more likely to identify what other people have done for you. If you've fostered a mindset of gratitude, you're likely to see that even though your child made a huge mess in the process, they made you breakfast to enjoy and you clean the kitchen appreciating their efforts instead of telling them that all they did was make more work for you. It allows you to feel closer to those in your family because you see the effort they put in and recognize that it deserves to be acknowledged. The more that you think in gratitude, the more positive your thoughts will become.

This works for children, as well. When you have two children fighting with each other, it can help a lot to pull them aside and have them each think of three things they like about the other person. Remembering the positives helps them to recognize that just because they're unhappy with someone in the moment doesn't mean that they have to be unhappy with them long-term or have a relationship ruined over it.

Even teens can benefit from gratitude, reminding them that while they may see other people with so much more, and while they may really want something that is given to other teens their age, they have to respect and acknowledge that your job is to provide them with food, shelter, and clothes. Much more beyond that is technically not a necessity and should be appreciated. You aren't obligated to provide your child with name-brand things or brand new cell phones. If you do, they're lucky. If not? They should appreciate what you're willing to do for them rather than assuming that you're obligated to do so.

If your home is currently lacking gratitude, you may notice a lot of tally keeping, tit-for-tat behaviors, and even people feeling like they shouldn't bother doing anything for each other. A family that doesn't recognize what everyone does for each other is a family that is going to struggle to support each other. Gratitude is essential, and will bring your entire household closer together.

Creating a House Focused on Gratitude

If you're just now realizing that gratitude is lacking in your home, there's no better time than now to start making the necessary changes. Your home is going to be stressed out. You're going to naturally have more conflicts until you're able to start making changes. However, bringing gratitude into your home doesn't have to be difficult. There are actually several very simple ways that you can bring that positivity back into your life, little by little. It might feel unnatural at first, but you'll soon come to realize that a genuine thank you to someone else for their effort is what counts. You'll recognize that the thought is what counts. While your child's card that was hand-drawn may look cheaper and noticeably less professional than one bought at the grocery store, the thought will be what counts. The effort that they chose to put into it is what matters.

When you acknowledge that the one truly limited resource in life is time, and that we give our time to other people willingly and freely so often, you start appreciating it more. Your child didn't have to spend an hour making you a card—they wanted to. You didn't have to work to pay to give your teen a phone at all—but you chose to. You sacrifice time to do things for other people, and that is deserving of gratitude. Likewise, when someone chooses to let the dog out for you, or to take care of the dishes so you don't have to, they're putting in effort to help you and that deserves recognition.

Remembering Manners

One easy way to emphasize gratitude is to reintroduce manners. It's easy to forego them when you've been around people long enough, or when you feel like you're in a position of power. Do you use your manners when you ask your children to do something? What about your partner? Do you remember to thank them afterward?

Manners remind us that what other people do is freely given. Even when you get to set the rules and say that your children must do chores, you need to acknowledge that technically, your children could still choose not to comply. There would be consequences, sure, but if you want their cooperation, please and thank you doesn't hurt.

For example, imagine that you need your teen to take the dog for a walk and then load the dishwasher after dinner. You could say, "Hey, go walk the dog and do the dishes," and walk away, but is your teen going to do it? They might—or they might not. Teens who feel disrespected may choose not to do so, even if they end up having to deal with the consequences later. A child who doesn't feel appreciated isn't going to really care to continue putting in efforts when their time is valuable and there are many other things they'd rather do.

Remembering to say please when asking someone to do something conveys that you recognize that what you're asking them to do isn't necessarily free from effort. You acknowledge that you're asking them to do something that will take up their time, no matter how much or how little.

Remembering your thank you's after someone has agreed to do something or after completing the task shows that you see that they put in the effort and you acknowledge that the effort that went into it was worth noticing. You're showing that you appreciate that they took a finite resource of their own and gave it to you, even if it was as simple as stopping something to hand you what you asked for.

Expressing Gratitude Each Day

One of the best ways to foster gratitude each day in your home is to recognize that something good happens each day. Try enforcing a moment each day, perhaps at dinner, where everyone talks about something they're grateful for that day. Maybe you're grateful that someone stopped to help you when you got a flat tire on your way to work. Maybe your child is grateful that you took an extra hour to cook their favorite meal for dinner. Maybe your teen is grateful that a friend helped them through a tough spot. Expressing gratitude each day shifts one's mindset toward recognizing those moments of importance. It helps to create an understanding of what went well and what didn't.

Fostering Gratitude in Conversations

Because your children will naturally follow your lead, one way to emphasize gratitude is to naturally slide it into conversations. For example, perhaps you're talking about working on getting your yard ready for spring planting and your teenager volunteers to help you till the garden beds and get them all ready for gardening. You could, for example, while talking about the garden, say that you really appreciate your teen's efforts. Later on, you may mention that the area they're working on looks good. By focusing on positive aspects throughout the time, you're able to create habitual acknowledgment of positivity. You're showing that there is plenty to be grateful for and that you see it.

Activities to Develop Gratitude in Children

If you want to develop gratitude in your children, a great starting point is to start packing it in whenever possible. Some small positive activities can be enough to get your child thinking in more positive terms and to start recognizing the power of gratitude.

Create a Gratitude Jar

A gratitude jar is a fun way to practice gratitude that is incredibly simple. So long as you have a jar, some art supplies, and pieces of paper that can be written on, you'll be able to create this activity quickly. All you need to do is encourage your child to decorate the jar in any way they choose to do so. Then, you add gratitude statements to it regularly. Generally, the recommended amount is three positive, grateful sentences per day, which then go into the jar.

If they choose to add more than three, then great! If they're struggling to find things they're grateful for, you can instead have them pull a few slips out to remind themselves of other things that they've appreciated in their days. You can have all sorts of statements as prompts for your child to fill in, such as:

- My favorite part of today was…
- I was really grateful for…
- I appreciate my friend…
- I felt really happy today when…
- I was proud today because…

- Something special about my family is...

Create a Gratitude Journal

As soon as your child is old enough to start writing, they can start creating gratitude journals as well. These are quite simple—your child will be taking the time to write down things they're grateful for each day. They don't have to be long, but by having a few things that were appreciated, a child can then think about why they liked or appreciated something. For example, perhaps your teen was appreciative of the fact that when she was having a really, really bad day, you took a sick day from work to support your child, calling it a mental health day. She may have greatly appreciated the effort.

Your younger child may be grateful that you let them choose out the kind of flowers that are growing in the front yard, or because the dog walking down the streep let them pet it. Anything could be a moment of gratitude.

Create Gratitude Cards

Another fun activity to help encourage children to be grateful is to encourage them to create gratitude cards. This is simple; it just requires them to write a quick card or letter to someone they love and who they appreciate. They may choose to write one to a friend or family member. They might write one to the neighbor across the street.

Gratitude cards can say whatever they want, so long as they're positive. They should include a thank you, an acknowledgment of what they appreciate, and why they appreciated it. Then, have them deliver the cards to who they were addressed to.

Activities to Develop Gratitude in Adults

Adults sometimes need reminders of gratitude as well. While you may not be intentionally avoiding using gratitude if you're forgetting it, you're going to be much less effective in your social interactions. It won't be as easy for you to see the positives in your relationships with other people if you're not able to recognize the help you get from other people.

Developing gratitude as an adult might take a bit more effort than it would to teach a child to learn it, but you do need to recognize it as essential to living a life more focused on positivity. If you want to be a positive individual, you'll need to be able to have gratitude when gratitude is due.

Mindful Reflection

Sometimes referred to as a gratitude meditation, to reflect mindfully is to be able to focus on positivity in your life. It is to recognize the ways that your life has been positive and to revel in that positivity for a period of time. It is to be able to acknowledge that you're having a good time, or that something positive has happened.

In mindful reflection, you will simply be looking at the things that you're grateful for in your life. You'll be allowing yourself to re-experience the appreciation that you feel toward other people. You can be grateful for the little things or the big things. Sometimes, it's just that one really good cup of coffee on your deck while you watch the sun rise one fine summer morning and you feel so happy to be alive. Other times, it may be to have a moment of quiet after you finally get an unruly, sick toddler to sleep, or the moment of gratitude of discovering that your tests for a disease are negative.

Your job in this instance is to allow yourself to relax and reflect upon those moments. You let yourself think about why you're appreciative of the moment, and how it makes you feel. You acknowledge that things could have been dramatically different if you weren't as lucky. By taking the time to reflect upon something that you're truly grateful for in the moment, you open your mind to positivity and gratitude.

Three Things Exercise

Just as you encourage your child to do with their own journals and gratitude jars, it's important that you can also acknowledge things that you're grateful for. You should be able to remind yourself of at least three things at the end of each day that you are grateful for. Even on horrendous days, you should be able to think of at least three things that help to bring you peace of mind. You may have had the worst day you've ever had, but when you pause and recognize that there are still things to be grateful for, you change your mindset.

Perhaps you're grateful for the fact that you're alive, and that you have a home. Maybe you're grateful that you had food to eat. You're reminding yourself that even on your worst days, there are other people who have it worse. It isn't meant to invalidate your feelings; it's meant to remind you that even if you had a bad day, there are still things worth appreciating.

Especially when we live in a world where so much pain exists or when we're so frustrated at the state of things, it can be easy to tell yourself that if you're not starving or dying—then you have nothing to complain about. No matter what your feelings of frustration are, you deserve to have them as well. The key here is also recognizing that no matter what your feelings, you should be able to see the positives as well. The positives generally remind you that, no matter how hard things may be in the moment, there are better times ahead to look forward to.

Mindfulness Ritual

If you've found yourself in a rut where you're constantly just doing what you need to do without ever actually doing something to live, you're going to have a hard time seeing the positives in the world around you. Your gratitude will be lacking because you're not really fully present enough to build the gratitude anywhere along the way. This is where mindfulness rituals come into play.

Mindfulness rituals are great because they can be changed endlessly to match whatever it is in the world that you're interested in. Maybe you choose to simply sit in the morning. Maybe you mindfully eat your breakfast. Maybe you have some other task, like showering or brushing your teeth, that you treat with the utmost mindfulness. Mindfulness will bring you back to the present. It will remind you to focus on the here and now, and as you do so, you can start being grateful for those little moments. You can be grateful that you have the opportunity to, for example, enjoy that little cup of coffee, or to be thankful that your shower you're taking is incredibly warm and comfortable.

When you choose a mindfulness ritual for yourself, it just has to be something that you do focused entirely on that moment. You should be able to be fully present in the moment the entire time that you're doing it so you can enjoy the moment. Find a ritual that works for you, and enjoy it every day. Let yourself be grateful for the little ritual that you use to keep yourself focused and feeling good. The more you do it, the easier it will become!

Final Words

Parenting is *hard*. Especially when you have no idea what the world your child will live in will look like, it can be hard to know what you should do to prepare them. What do they need to know? Will they need to know how to cook and sew? What about pay bills? of course, these are basics that anyone should know how to do—but what can you do to prepare your child with in order to be a successful, resilient person?

As you read through this book, you gained the keys to happiness for any well-adjusted individual. You don't have to raise the next rockstar or the next Nobel Prize winner. What you do need to do is raise someone who is capable of thinking clearly and calmly, and who is able to control their own emotions. You want to raise someone who will have the mentality to endure a lifetime of roadblocks, obstacles, and difficulties. Life isn't perfect. You can't expect things to go perfectly all of the time, but you can give your children the tools they'll need to cope when the going gets tough.

As you start changing your home life, little by little, you'll start getting all sorts of signs that it's working. Perhaps your children act a little more positively when they're struggling. Maybe you see ways that you could have changed your own behaviors in a situation to be more conducive to fostering a good reaction. However, no matter who you are and how you parent, one thing is for sure: Your child will look up to you. They will naturally feel the need to emulate you and to recognize the strength you represent. They'll want to follow in your footsteps, whether that's in creating sustainable habits or introducing positivity and gratitude into their life. No matter what you choose to do, if you're able to start implementing and fostering the seven habits that you've been introduced to, you're going to find that positivity and healthy mindsets are closer than you think.

Developing a child who is adaptable and resilient takes time. It takes careful cultivation of your child's confidence. Raising a child who is capable of recognizing that they can always improve and that they can always keep trying to achieve their goals will raise children who are big thinkers and will continue to get up every time the world knocks them back down again. Teaching your child to be self-compassionate reminds them that they deserve a little grace every now and then when they make a mistake as well. They wouldn't judge other people for making mistakes—why should they judge themselves? Encouraging mindfulness builds the ability your child needs to be able to cope with negativity and to develop self-control essential for emotional regulation. They recognize that they are not alone in their pain. Creativity teaches your child to be a problem-solver and a go-getter, not afraid of any obstacles that stand in their way. Sustainability ensures that your child is taking care of the world that takes care of him or her. Finally, gratitude teaches them to see that there is positivity in just about any situation if you look hard enough. There's always something to be grateful for in the world, and happiness will be found when you're willing to identify and acknowledge that point.

With these seven skills that you can pass on to your child, you prepare them for a lifetime of positivity. You prepare them for a lifetime of being able to feel capable of taking on the world, no matter what may come. Though the world will change, those abilities that your child needs to cope will remain the same, and these skills will ensure your child is ready to tackle even the largest mountains in the future.

Thank You!

I would like to start by thanking each of you for reading *Are You Parenting the Adult of the Future?* It would mean the world to me, as the author, if you could take time to post an Amazon review. Hearing real feedback from real readers helps any writer improve their craft!

I wish you all a beautiful and bright future ahead!

Printed in Great Britain
by Amazon